I0006668

Lucky
That Way

*Stories of Seizing the Moment
While Creating the Games Millions Play*

Brad Fregger

Austin, Texas

Lucky That Way
By Brad Fregger
Copyright Brad Fregger, 2012
Groundbreaking Press
8306 Arboles Circle
Austin, Texas 78737
www.groundbreaking.com

Second Edition

ISBN : 978-0-9773535-3-8

Senior Editor
Barbara Foley

Editorial Assistance
Lee Moczygemba
Judy Mazarin
Jon Fregger
Martha Fregger

Cover and Interior Design and Production
Dan'l Terry

All rights reserved. No part of this book may be reproduced or utilized in any form or by any means, electronic, or mechanical, including photocopying or recording, or by any information storage and retrieval system, without the permission in writing from the author.

To

My Grandchildren
Tony, Noah, Ryan, Erika, Ainsley, Smith & Alex

&
My Adopted Grandson
Adnan Barqawi

&
My Great Granddaughter
Lila

This book was originally written in 1998 and it was my first. In the past 13 years I have written six additional books and played thousands more computer games (mostly sudoku, poker, *Nanosaur 2*, and *Angry Birds),* most recently on my iPhone and Barbie's iPad.

After all these years not a month goes by when I'm not asked where someone can buy *Solitaire Royale* or *Ishido*. In addition, there is a real fan base for *Seize the Day*; in fact, many of the *Seize the Day* images are once again available in all of their full animation beauty.

You can find additional information on *Ishido, Seize the Day,* and *Heaven & Earth* on Ian Gilman's website (www.iangilman.com). In fact, he is giving away some versions of *Ishido* and *Heaven & Earth.* Thank you, Ian, for keeping these games alive. I'm sorry to have to report that *Solitaire Royale* has disappeared into the past; I couldn't convince anyone to do a new version of this much-loved game.

In recent years I have been delighted with the development of the iPhone and the wonderful game applications that are a true reminder of the "good old days" of computer gaming. I never got into first-person shooters and sports games (except for computer golf), so the advent of the iPhone's compelling games has been a blessing for me.

This book is basically a memoir of my years in the computer game industry. This was the beginning of an exciting adventure in creativity and innovation. We hadn't yet discovered what the big sellers were going to be, so we were free to create anything that we could convince marketing to take a chance on.

I was especially fortunate to be the first person in the world to hold the title of Computer Game Producer. The story of how this happened is included in this book. Soon after, my peers at Activision were also given this title. (They had previously been called project managers.) Then Electronic Arts quickly followed suit.

I became an extremely successful Computer Game Producer with some of the most successful and longest-lasting computer games in the world. I am very proud to have been the producer for *Shanghai* (developed by Brodie Lockard), one of the most successful games of all time (you may know it as computer Mahjong); and the creator of the very first commercial version of computer card solitaire, *Solitaire Royale*. (Computer card solitaire is recognized as the most played game in the world.) The stories of these games, as well as many others, are in this book.

I truly hope that you will enjoy reading my stories about the beginnings of the computer entertainment industry. I am in awe of how far the industry has come in the past 30 years. *Pitfall 2* was the breakout computer entertainment product in 1982, the first game to use 8K of computer memory. Then, I produced the C64 and Atari 800 versions, truly the top-of-the-line computer entertainment products of that time. As recently as 15 years ago, while developing the Jack Nicklaus computer-golf game, we couldn't do realistic water (although we did do a top-of-the-line 3D computer figure). Now, we have the movie *Avatar* ... with water so real, it's truly awesome.

That's all for now. Thanks for buying *Lucky That Way*, and I hope you enjoy reading it ... I know I enjoyed living it!

Brad Fregger
Austin, Texas
February, 2012

Seize
the
Moment

Preface

I became deeply involved in the computer entertainment business in 1981. I was forty-one years old, just starting in an industry that was destined to be controlled by people not much more than half my age. When I was at Activison, from 1983 to 1986, I was actually the oldest member of management in the company. Several years later when I joined Eclipse Entertainment, they introduced me by announcing, "This is Brad. He started designing games back when they used sticks and wrote in the dirt."

Lucky That Way is a selection of stories and lessons from those years. These stories show how my philosophy of *seizing the moment* made things easier, even made the seemingly impossible, possible. It was a wonderful ride, truly a time when I was able to spend my life doing my work and not working at my job.

Everything in this book actually happened...although some of it may seem unbelievable. And it all happened to one person...me! Such is life, often stranger than fiction.

That being said, it's only fair to tell you the dialogue presented is not verbatim. I didn't have a tape recorder with me when the incidents occurred, and my memory is not that sharp!

Some names were changed in the stories. This was done for three reasons: first, to protect the guilty (there were also times when I chose not to protect them), second, to protect the innocent (when I deemed this necessary), and third, because I couldn't remember the person's name, or find it through research. However, if you find yourself in one of these stories and want to be identified correctly, drop me a note and I'll make the correction in the next edition.

My Email address is: brad@groundbreaking.com

This book has been a blast to write. Here's hoping you find it as much fun to read and that you gain something from it to carry with you for the rest of your life.

Brad Fregger
Austin, Texas
November, 1998

LUCKY THAT WAY

Contents

AFTERWORD

by
Orson Scott Card

Foreword

When I went to college in 1968, part of freshman orientation was to show us the computer that handled registration for the whole campus of twenty thousand students. It filled a room.

In the 1970s, we began to hear rumors of computers small enough and cheap enough that regular people could buy them. I coveted a Wang word processor, but wanted a computer that could do other things as well. My first computer was an Altos CP/M machine with two eight-inch floppies. I ran WordStar in 64K of memory, and it was a miracle. It cost $10,000 for computer, terminal, and printer.

We soon bought an MP/M Altos so that my wife and I could each have terminals on the same computer. But prices had already fallen enough that this system, with two terminals and a ten-megabyte hard drive, cost the same amount.

I wanted portability; we bought the first model of the Osborne. I actually carried that sewing machine through airports and worked on that four-inch screen. The PCjr. Several Toshiba laptops. We soon found that the ideal system cost $3,000. Then $2,000. Our NEC Spinwriter was replaced by an

HP LaserJet. We got color with an Epson Stylus. The 300 baud modem with which I first signed on to Delphi in 1983 is now replaced by a 33000 bps modem that takes us everywhere. In my house we have a half-dozen computers linked together as a network, and every one of them gets used almost every day.

But for me, and many like me, all the serious uses for computers are just an excuse to buy a machine that will let us play games.

The saga of computer games follows a different trajectory. It was that first *Pong* game we played at the university student center. Then *Breakout*, which was the first solo game that I got completely addicted to. *Asteroids* and *Space Invaders* and a slew of other space games, leading to *Galaxians* and then *Galaga*, where for months I held the high score on the machine in the Seven-Eleven down the hill from our house in South Bend, Indiana.

Donkey Kong, *PacMan*, an Olympics simulation in 1984 - my coins dropped into the slots year after year. Because the arcades always had games a little better, a little faster than anything I could get on my computer at home.

But that computer at home - I'm not talking about my Altos. That was for serious work, for writing. I didn't have that serious machine for long before I walked into a computer store and saw the machine of my dreams: An Atari that would let me play Breakout at home.

I couldn't pretend, in those days, that I was buying it for work. My wife knew that I already had a very expensive work computer that cost more than any car we would own for many years. The Atari would not be for work. It was, pure and simple, a machine for play. Oh, I talked about learning to program, and I meant it - but even that was going to be play. What could I ever do that was serious and useful with that

Atari?

The answer: Nothing.

I bought the Atari 400, with the maximum extra memory you could put in it. But I soon found that loading games on tape was inconvenient, and saving programs I was writing was even more annoying. I had to have a disk drive. I needed two cartridge slots. So I spent $800 on an Atari 800, and the same amount again on the disk drive. I began to buy and play games that were too big to fit on a cartridge. I began to program seriously, staying up all night even though I had classes in grad school the next day. From Atari BASIC I graduated to writing machine language for routines that had to run fast - and I mean machine language, not assembler code. I didn't own an assembler. I figured out the hex values of the machine-code commands and used BASIC to POKE them into memory and run them.

I bought magazines like *Compute!* and typed in the programs that looked interesting. Can you imagine buying software these days by typing it in, line by line? But we did it back then, because the machines were small and slow, so programs had to be tight. I remember figuring out ways to do a routine in five lines, then four, then three, and then - ah, the ultimate elegance - a single line of code! Programming itself was a great game.

From reading *Compute!* I learned of a job opening as a book editor; soon I was in Greensboro, North Carolina, helping move the book publishing division of Compute! into new areas. I wrote articles; I wrote programs; I edited other people's articles and rewrote their sloppy programs into quick, elegant, bug-free tight ones. It was a lot more fun editing software than editing language, because in the end, the software either ran or it didn't. You knew when it was exactly right.

Because I worked there, I was forced to use Commodore machines as well as Ataris. The Commodore 64 had no more usable memory than the Atari 800, but because the extra RAM was physically present, they advertised it like crazy and outsold the Atari, even though the Commodore machines always looked really bad on television screens, while the Atari graphics chip - the Antic - was crisp, clear, and readable. The Atari was far and away the better machine. But aggressive pricing and advertising that depended on the ignorance of the consumer did for Commodore what the same practices did for VHS videotape: the second-rate machine beat up the quality machine in the marketplace.

Then the IBM PC, a miserable, deliberately crippled computer that was nowhere near as good as the Atari 800, swept away all the competition - the Commodore, the Atari, and all the serious CP/M machines as well - and became the standard for no better reason than that everyone in business knew you could never get fired for buying IBM (that was then, this is now). Instead of the vast freedom of the 6502 chip, in which the entire zero page served as almost 256 registers, programmers were limited to only eight, and machine code wasn't fun to write anymore. Also, graphics were primitive - monochrome or four colors (one of them black); on the PCjr, a mere sixteen.

I hated the PC. I did write one book on graphics for the PCjr, and wrote an atlas program that had one feature I was really proud of - you could cycle through every presidential election in US history and see a map showing you which state voted for which party. (I still haven't seen an atlas program that does that!) But the PCjr died before the book could be published. No one but my family has ever seen the program. I no longer worked for *Compute!* I wrote a cool music program for the Atari that ran in the interrupts, but that never got published either. The computer world had passed me by. I haven't even tried to write a program in a dozen years. The day of the amateur - or at least of the middle-aged amateur who had to make a living - was over.

But I still played the games. And so did my kids. Early on, when my son would get angry at the way arcade-based games were designed to defeat him, I wrote my own games for the kids, nonthreatening, simple games that they had a great time with. Later, though, commercial programs began to create games that were far more interesting than anything the arcades could offer.

Because I was a writer, I got a gig writing game reviews. People sent them to me for free. Cool. There could be no better job on earth.

A lot of the genres of computer games left me cold. I never understood the appeal of flight simulators. It looked to me like paying a lot of money and spending a lot of time doing a simulated version of a really boring job. Nor did the kick-boxing games that were taking over the arcades thrill me at all.

What I played were games with a story to them. For a while I played fantasy games where you wandered the world, battling enemies while trying to achieve heroic goals - I enjoyed those until they became nothing but 3-D blastfests as boring as the combat games in the arcades. I have friends who are addicted to *Duke Nukem* and I can see that its humor makes it better than the grimmer competition, but I've never wanted to sit down and play it.

What really worked for me were the history games. Not battle simulations - those were too rigidly structured, and they were only about war, which gets way too grim and destructive for me, all about winning or losing. No, I wanted the games where you build nations or grow cities or colonize new worlds, where you build alliances and use a mix of strategy and tactics to beat skillful computer opponents.

The first such game I played was *Romance of the Three Kingdoms*, from Koei Software. I played it over and over again for a couple of years. It consumed my life, taking me through many all-nighters. The better I knew the game, the more I loved it. I would set myself challenges: Can I win without getting Sima Yi as my leading general? Can I become the unifier of China starting from this weak little province?

The funny thing is that the gamewrights didn't understand their own game - they didn't know what made it work. They thought it was the simulation aspect that was fun, so when they created a game called *Genghis Khan*, they made it so "realistic" that it was tedious to play. In a review, I exaggerated the tedium by saying that the game only lacked a good "walking" simulation - you make the character take each step by pressing the L and R keys alternately, and if you ever pressed the same key three times in a row, the character would fall down (pressing the same key twice just made the character skip merrily along).

But because I wrote a mocking review of a bad game, the publisher punished me by not sending me the next game they came out with. I came from the world of fiction publishing, where bad reviews are almost as good as good reviews - when you're standing there in the bookstore, chances are you'll see the book and think, "I've read something about that," and you pick it up and look at the jacket copy and ... maybe you buy it. But game publishing was an immature industry. The marketing people didn't know how to deal with bad reviews, didn't know how to take them philosophically. I once had people from Microprose come to Greensboro and take me out to dinner; I finally realized that the whole reason for this visit was because they wanted to persuade me to like their games. I had to laugh and tell them, If you want me to write better reviews of your games, publish better games! And this from a company that had got more rave reviews from me than any other! They just didn't get it - nobody in the business did. The only bad review is the one that doesn't mention your game but talks about your competitor. The only bad review is silence.

And some of the gamewrights were as bad as the marketing people. Chris Crawford, for instance, who was one of the best of the war-simulation gamewrights, took such umbrage at my review of his laughably unrealistic world-politics simulation game that he not only sent me a letter that proved he still didn't have a clue what I was talking about, but also proceeded to block anyone who tried to invite me to computer game conferences, or so I've been told. Talk about thin-skinned! If he ever got a killer review like some of those I've been given for my fiction, there'd probably be casualties.

With *Romance of the Three Kingdoms*, I began to experience full-fledged addiction. I'd been hooked on some arcade games before - computer and pinball- but the need for quarters put a ceiling on the amount of playing I could do. And *Breakout* had been pretty addictive as a home game, as well. *Romance*, though, stole hours, days, weeks of my life. I finally quit only when I got hooked on another game. There have been a whole series of games that filled the same need, if that's what it is, that *Romance* filled for me - most of them by Sid Meier: *Railroad Tycoon*, *Civilization*, *Colonization*.

There was another game, though. One that was nothing like *Romance of the Three Kingdoms*. A game that arguably transformed the culture of computing, making every computer user a game player, even at work, even on those serious machines. And that game was *Solitaire Royale*.

Solitaire - the real game, with real cards - had been part of my life since childhood. Being devout Christians, of course, we never had those evil face cards in our house; instead, we played all the same games using Rook cards. My family was completely aware of the hypocrisy involved in doing so; we admitted it and continued to enjoy playing. To me, though, the only solitaire was the one my parents taught, played the way they played it. *Solitaire Royale* did not follow the same rules, and at first that really annoyed me.

After all, since solitaire is a game you play alone, the rules are whatever you say they are! So why shouldn't I be able, in the computer version, to follow my family's rule that when only five or fewer cards were left in your hand, you could open it up and draw any of them? Of course, the computer couldn't easily be programmed to allow rule changes. And at least I could change card decks - a really nice feature of the graphics of the game.

I got over the frustration quickly, though, because *Solitaire Royale* was actually many different solitaire games, most of which were completely new to me, and most of which I enjoyed a great deal. In fact, we even started playing some of them with real cards, when we were at the beach, for instance. The piece de resistance of *Solitaire Royale*, however, was "Aunt Anne's Tour," which consisted of playing each of the games in order and recording your combined score from all of them on a vanity board.

The importance of vanity boards in computer games cannot be overstated. The ability to put up your name where others can see it - or even where you alone will see it later, and have a goal to surpass the next time you play - becomes an important part of the enjoyment of the game. Aunt Anne's Tour became the family game. For my wife began playing *Solitaire Royale* as well - the first computer game she had ever become addicted to. (This actually did wonders for family solidarity, since she could now understand something about my madness in playing when it made no sense to play.)

In fact, *Solitaire Royale* was so well designed - and was written with such rock-solid code - that it is now the oldest game still playable on our computers at home. It helps, of course, that it had no copy protection. We bought several copies of the game, because we try to be fair, but there are some programs that would have stayed on our computers except that the copy protection scheme meant that every time we upgraded the computer, we had to reinstall the game - and sometimes couldn't even do that unless we remember first to uninstall the previous installation. With all the copy-protected games, we eventually just bagged them and went on. Kind of a shame, though - I would probably still play *Lode Runner*, for instance, but you had to slide that 5-1/4-inch disk into the drive in order to play it, and I don't think there's a drive that size on any computer in the house.

Certainly not on my laptop!

But *Solitaire Royale* did everything right. I played a round of Aunt Anne's Tour last night.

And the book you hold in your hands is the memoire of the man who, as much as anyone, caused *Solitaire Royale* to exist.

❦

Brad Fregger didn't program *Solitaire Royale*. He didn't draw up the graphics. But he can still claim to be one of the creators of the game, because he was the driving force behind its existence and its marketing.

Computer gaming is like film and drama, in that it is generally not a solitary art. Now, to tell the truth, neither is publishing. When I write a novel, I need to send it to my editor and publisher - and for most of my books, that means Beth Meacham as editor and Tom Doherty as publisher. And if my audience is able to find my books, it's because Beth did a good job of putting the physical package together, finding just the right cover for the book; and it's because Tom is a marvelous marketer of books, one of the rare publishers who actually reads the books he sells, and a man who understands both the business and the public so well that he could start up a new paperback house in the 1980s, an era of conglomerates, not entrepreneurial startups, and make it a dominant force in several genres within only a few years.

So I know about the importance of the business and marketing side of the arts - that's how the artist is able to find an audience.

But in drama, film, television, and computer games, the role of the business side is far more important than in publishing. I write the book I want to write. If no one buys it, it won't bankrupt anybody, unless they overprinted.

In film, though, when you spend ten million bucks on a film and it tanks, you're dead, unless it was somebody else's money. That's why film is dominated by studios - they have enough money to absorb some losses, covering them with income generated by the hits (and fudged out of other people's share of those hits by creative accounting methods - but that's another book).

The big frustration in film, however, is that nobody knows what's going to hit. And when a film does make a billion dollars, no one understands exactly why it did. Still, they try to limit their risk by trying to imitate the hits in some way. They try to figure out the formula, and buy scripts that fit the formula (but most of those fail). Or they hire the same star who was in the last hit - only to find that it wasn't the star after all. Or they hire the same director. Or the same writer. Or they film a sequel to the hit, hoping to dip twice into the same well.

Computer games work on the Hollywood model, though no one understood that at first. Since games were "published," people tried to handle them like the book business at the beginning. Somebody writes a game and then a publisher brings it out. And sometimes games still work that way. The *Castle Wolfenstein* guys wrote their games out of love and distributed them as shareware before they went big time. *Myst* was a garage game, as I understand it.

Most of the time, though, in order to create a game you've got to have a lot of the money put together up front, so you can pay the artist and programmer to work full time on the project. And that means you've got to get risk capital up front, and somebody's got to tend that money to make sure it's wisely spent and that the programmer and artist working on the game do their job. In other words, you've got to have a producer.

Brad Fregger was present at the changeover from the publishing model to the producing model. That's part of what this book is about. And, just as in the movies, this book is about the frustrating fact that even if you create the best game in the world, that doesn't mean some slacker can't rip off the idea and put you out of business. Or some big-money studio — er, pardon me, software company — can't string you along, using up your money, and then stiff you at the last second. I'm not going to try to tell you that story. That's Brad's job. Heck, I'm not even going to tell you the story of how Brad and I met. He tells it better.

What I will tell you is this: In publishing, there's a clear line between the creative people and the business people. The writer creates the book; the publisher and editor clean it up, package it, sell it. There are cases where the editor and even the publisher are more helpful (or more intrusive) than that, but the line is generally clear and firm.

But in computer games, as in film and television, there is no such line. Oh, they talk about "the talent," but they still know perfectly well that the driving force behind most projects is the producer. Even a project driven by a director or writer or actor is still producer driven, because in those cases the director, writer, or actor is the producer, or one of the producers. They are making it happen, putting it together, getting money and story together, getting distribution lined up. Getting it made, and then getting it sold.

So when a film wins best picture, it's not an accident, it's not remotely unfair, that it's not the star or the director or the writer who goes up to get the Oscar or the Golden Globe or the Emmy. It's the producer. And if you see the star or director or writer up there, it's because he or she also worked as a producer on the project.

That's whom you're meeting here in these pages - a producer of those bits of interactive art called computer games. He's not part of a big studio, he's an independent. And he's had some misses and some disastrous experiences, with no one there to cushion the fall. The programmer got paid. The artist got paid. But as often as not, the producer didn't get a dime, or lost money. The hits made it worthwhile. No, more than that - even the failures were worthwhile, because he loves having caused a game to come into existence.

I said earlier that *Solitaire Royale* may well have changed computer culture and turned even serious computers into game machines. That isn't because everybody plays Solitaire Royale, of course. Most computer users have never heard of it.

The change, like most changes, was vectored through Microsoft.

Microsoft is, of course, Satan. It is precisely the company that anti-trust laws were invented in order to prevent. Microsoft has never, not once in its history, never created anything new. Every single idea that has made Microsoft such a monster - from MSDOS to Windows, from Excel to Word to Explorer to ... to everything - has been copied from other people, and usually isn't as good. Few Microsoft products would ever have won in the marketplace on merit alone. But just like Rockefeller's Standard Oil, if it can't beat a competitor, it buys it; if it can't buy it, it beats it. It steals what it can get away with stealing, and when it can't, it pays a license fee until it can buy the company that owns the copyright. And when some company does something wonderful and innovative, it incorporates a second-rate copy of it into Windows and wipes the other company off the map. Just ask the folks who made Stacker and Norton Desktop about Microsoft.

And then to add insult to injury, people listen to Bill Gates talk about the future as if he had anything to do with creating it. Bill Gates doesn't innovate. Bill Gates only knows how to take what the real innovators created and make all the money from it without actually earning it himself. We'll let the Justice Department decide what we'll call the process they actually use.

In the meantime, though, like it or not, Microsoft rules the world of computing.

So when *Solitaire Royale* was a hit, Microsoft saw and Microsoft understood: This uncopyprotected game based on a public domain concept was so easy to steal that they could almost do it in their sleep.

When Windows 3.0 appeared, every copy included a free

Solitaire game.

It was nowhere near as good as *Solitaire Royale*. But it was free. And people could play it at work for a couple of minutes — in a break, during a phone call (if only Bill Clinton had had Windows running on his desk), after finishing the deadline project, or instead of working on the deadline project — there's always time for a Solitaire game.

This gave rise to a whole new genre of games - I call them "nuisance games." They all can be played in a few minutes. You don't think you're going to play them for long, but you end up playing them again and again and again until you wonder where the day went, or the week. They're fun and quick and they can ruin your life, if you're an addict.

Take *Tetris*, for instance - and Brad Fregger nearly did! When you're addicted to this game (which suffers from the arcade-game structure in which you eventually get to levels so fast that you physically cannot beat them), you begin to see the shapes moving across your field of vision even when you're not playing. This is so scary that I gave up *Tetris* except for an occasional game now and then. It's just too weird to be giving a speech or having a conversation or teaching a class, seeing shapes moving down your field of vision even though you know they're not there!

For me, though, the best of the nuisance games are played with cards or tiles. All the solitaire games you find in the Windows Entertainment Pack owe their existence to *Solitaire Royale* - games like *Freecell* and *Cruel* are legitimate solitaire games in their own right, but Microsoft packaged them and put them out as nuisance games only because *Solitaire Royale* proved that people wanted games like that.

And the tile games, too, began with Brad Fregger's projects. When you play *Taipei* on your Windows machine (and I do), it's good to remember that it was ripped off from Brad Fregger's *Shanghai* project. But, once again, you should read the story as Brad tells it.

Computers have become small worlds that we live in. We leave one world - the world with people and money and families, the world with toilets and dinners and sex and sleep and kleenex and dishes and all those mundane details - and we enter another, where people are words in a chat room and we can have the most marvelous adventures and play the most amazing games without ever stirring out of our chairs.

There are ways in which the computer world is horrible, making us even more sedentary than television already did, cutting us off from the real world. But there are also ways in which the computer world is wonderful, letting us have experiences we could never have in real life - and safely! - while we meet fascinating (and boring) people we would never have met in life, send letters at the press of a button, create freely and play marvelously.

I could live without computers. I really could. Sometimes, for days at a time, I do.

But I don't want to live without computers. I want to be in the place where people like Brad Fregger will give me a new experience from time to time. Take me to a new place, give me a new way to think or a new memory or a new puzzle.

And, because I've read Brad Fregger's memoire, *Lucky That Way*, I now know something about what it's like to be the producer. To make things happen. To put things together. I'm not that kind of guy myself. But Brad Fregger is, and I'm glad this book has given me a chance to know him and his work a little better.

Orson Scott Card
Greensboro NC
3 November 1998

Thanks

During the time the experiences shared in this book took place, I was living with a wonderful woman, my wife for 37 years, Kathie Fregger. I want to thank her for the support and affirmation she gave me during that time, for being so understanding and loving. We have three wonderful children, who with their spouses have given us seven terrific grandchildren.

In 1996 I experienced a major "mid-life crisis" and found I had to leave and strike out on my own. This was a tough time for me. Then surprise of all surprises, I met and fell in love with Barbara Foley. In many ways she saved my life. We were engaged in February of 1998, and we'll be married early in 1999.

Barbara has been a tremendous support during the writing of this book, providing both editing expertise and inspiration. I'm not sure I could have written it without her.

Others also helped, not the least of which were my parents, Rolly and Martha Fregger; and my children, Jeff, Jon and Bryn, who had to put up with listening to me read chapters out loud. My dear friend, Beth Pole, provided the miracle quote in the first chapter.

Initial copies of *Lucky That Way* were

sent to some close friends who were very helpful in getting the facts straight. And many others answered questions and added recollections of their own. Thank you: Dick and Diana Aldrich, Ron Berlin, Greg Walberg, Mike Franco, Sherry Whiteley-Roach, Dick Lehrberg, Gordon Walton, Tim Fields, David Stafford, Stephen Balkum, Mike and Paula Sandige, Carol Manley, and Happy Keller.

The book's final look was handled by a great group of people who helped me keep the writing tight and easy to read, while making sure I dotted all my i's and crossed all my t's. Thank you for your wonderful edit of this book: Lee Moczygemba, Judy Mazarin, Jon Fregger, Martha Fregger, and, of course, Barbara Foley. The cover is the creation of Dan'l Terry, one of the finest 3D artists in the world today.

Barbara gets the credit for finding our publisher, Sunstar Publishing, Ltd. in Fairfield, Iowa. Rodney Charles, the Managing Editor, has been a joy to work with. I wish with all my heart every author could find a publisher as wonderful.

Finally, I want to thank Orson Scott Card for the Foreword. Actually it's an essay on the history of computers and computer games as seen through his eyes. This was a gift way beyond my expectation.

Thank you, everyone! I am truly blessed to be able to share this life with you.

B F.

Seize the Moment   Chapter 1

Seizing the moment is what this book is about. You've heard of Carpe Diem — Seize the Day! Well, the first step after deciding to seize the day, is to learn to *seize the moment.*

When you learn to *seize the moment,* when you learn to accept into your life the unplanned, the unknown, coincidence, synchronicity, serendipity, and even miracles, everything gets easier!

This reminds me of a favorite story that demonstrates *seizing the moment* very well.

It seems there was a rich man who had two sons. One son, James, was extremely optimistic, always saw the half-filled glass as having the potential of being full. The other son, William, very pessimistic, always saw the same glass as becoming empty.

The rich man decided to test just how much his sons personified these divergent points of view, so he prepared two rooms full of surprises, one for each son. For William he gave a room full of all of the most wonderful toys in the world, and for James he gave a room full of horse manure.

About an hour after each son had entered his room, the rich man visited each in turn.

When he opened the door to William's room he saw him sitting in the middle of the floor crying.

"I'm so sad," William cried.

"How can you be sad in the midst of all of these wonderful toys?" the rich man asked.

"I can't stop thinking that someday I will either grow tired of them or they'll get broken and then I'll have nothing to play with," he wailed.

The rich man shook his head and left to see how James was faring.

Upon opening James' door he saw him digging through the horse manure with a big smile on his face and a song on his lips.

Curious, the rich man interrupted, "Why are you so happy my son?"

"Oh Daddy, there's so much horse manure...**there's just got to be a pony in here someplace!**"

James had a natural ability to look for "ponies" even when it appeared he was facing nothing but horse manure. He knew how to *seize the moment.*

Lucky That Way takes place during fifteen of the years I've been involved in the computer games industry. I was extremely lucky; lucky to have produced a couple of the most successful computer games in history; and lucky to have been able to work with some of the most talented people in the industry.

I don't want you to think I've walked through life, from one wonderful experience to another, with no problems or hardships. I remember one time in particular when I had been promoted to West Coast Merchandise Manager/Men's Clothing Buyer for a chain of women's wear stores, Foxmoor Casuals. This was during a time in my life when I didn't know what I didn't know and, even more important, I didn't know what I did know. In my immaturity I reacted by acting macho and becoming a jerk. The ultimate result: I was fired and given no severance. I was literally out in the street, with a wife and three children at home to support.

After the initial shock and the great embarrassment had passed, I picked myself up, dusted myself off, and started all over again. I took control of my life; I made the decision to *seize the moment.*

I'm not talking about "living for the moment" which is an entirely different thing. To "live for the moment" means to not accept responsibility for your life; it means to "go with the flow" in a lackadaisical way. When you live this way, you don't make plans, you don't have goals, you drift from one day to the next. You never seize the day, let alone the moment.

In addition, I'm not talking about touchy feely stuff; I'm talking about business. I'm talking about getting difficult things done. I'm talking about accomplishing the impossible!

I've spent the last fifteen years developing computer software, over one hundred products in total. Products I was responsible for have sold millions of copies world-wide and have become the most successful, most played, in the world. In all that time I *never* failed to finish a product. This was in an industry where the all-too-often uncompleted products have their own name – vaporware.

And in an industry where late, budget destroying product is the rule, not the exception, my products have consistently been on time and on budget.

This record of accomplishment is exceptional in the software industry, and is in no small part due to my commitment to *seizing the moment.* I like to believe I can hear opportunity when she's only lightly scratching at the door. Or to quote a very dear friend of mine..."I don't believe in miracles, I depend on them."

❧

It all started at Atari during the beginnings of video games and personal computers. Initially, video games took 4k of memory, such a tiny amount. Now computer games take 400 Meg of memory. There's 1000k in 1 Meg, 400,000k in 400 Meg. This means games today are 100,000 times bigger. They aren't

100,000 times more fun, or more challenging; but they are better in some significant ways. And the potential for the future is extremely exciting.

This book tells stories about computer games, but it's really about much more than that. It's about people, creativity, commitment, motivation, getting things done. You will read about skilled professionals, who are driven to push the envelop, to try something that has never been done before; individuals who are inherently curious about how things work, and how they can be made to work better and do more. These people don't need to be managed; in fact, some of them are unmanageable. But, if you can point them in the right direction, they will accomplish the extremely difficult and apologize for not doing it better or faster.

Years ago, when I was leaving Activision, Ken Coleman, the VP of Product Development, and I went out for drinks and conversation after work one day. We sat there discussing numerous things, my plans, the company, the good times we had. At one point in the conversation, Ken looked over at me and said, "In twenty words or less, what does it take to deliver quality product on budget and on time?"

I thought for a moment and said, "Find the right people, show them how good they are, and then get out of their way."

"Is that it?" he asked.

"You did say twenty words or less..." He motioned me to continue. "Make sure they're heading in the same direction. And make sure they stay on course. That's it."

"Basically it sounds pretty simple," he said.

"Most important stuff is," I said. "The problem is in the implementation and staying out of their way."

Finding the right people and keeping them motivated is the real key to successful product development, successful completion of any program or product. It is also one of the most difficult things to do.

Joe Kipper was the manager of the Sears store in Mountain View, California, in the same shopping center where I managed a successful men's wear store. I was in my mid-twenties, young to be a store manager, and for some reason, Joe decided to take me on, mentor me, even though I didn't work for Sears. We had a great friendship.

After Mountain View, Joe went to the Arden Fair store in Sacramento. It was there, that he and his staff won "Profit Store of the Year" for two years in a row. When you win that kind of an award, it's presented by the Sears CEO.

After the award ceremony, Joe rode back to the airport with him in the limo. They were discussing the store and what a fine example it was, when he said to Joe, "You know, that's an impressive team you've got there."

"Thank you," Joe responded.

"You know, Joe..." he said in a conspiratorial tone, "with a team like that, anyone could have the best profit store in the chain."

After a moment's thought, Joe said, "Yep, I've always been lucky that way."

Yep, Joe and I have always been *lucky that way!*

As I said earlier, this book contains many stories which illustrate *seizing the moment* and everything that is meant by that simple phrase. It's about coincidence, synchronicity, serendipity, even small miracles.

It's about overcoming impossible odds, not giving in to defeat even in the face of tremendous adversity. It's about getting kicked in the face when you're already down, but still getting up to start over again and again. It's about winning, but not always winning big; and it's about success, but not always major financial success.

Some of the stories I share are of coincidence, synchronicity or serendipity. These terms describe the same types of events, but have important, subtle differences. To clarify, let me tell you how I define these terms and the differences between them.

Coincidence is pure accident and is often understood only as coincidence after the fact.

Synchronicity is not accident. One definition I like is "meaningful coincidence." Basically, for me, synchronicity occurs when I have a goal in mind; and an unexplainable coincidence or series of coincidences takes place that allows the goal to be realized. Desire and realization come together in a way that seems miraculous, beyond our ability to make it happen.

Here is a story about synchronicity, about "meaningful coincidence." Some thirty odd years ago I was reading everything I could find on the subject of soul travel. This is a "skill" some people seem to have that enables them to leave their bodies and travel consciously to other places in their "soul body." Every book I found listed in its bibliography four books that were considered to be the foundation of the belief. I couldn't find them in the Mountain View Library, the San Jose Library or any other library in Santa Clara County, including the Stanford Library. I decided to quit looking and leave it up to a greater consciousness.

The next day, I had an intense compulsion to go to the Los Altos Library and obtain a library card. The need was so great I left work immediately and drove to the library.

While the card was being typed by the librarian, a young man, about fourteen years old, showed me a letter from the Dali Lama.

I asked, "Do you study Tibet and their religion?"

"My family has always studied this type of thing. My dad has many books on psychic phenomena, mysticism, religions, all kinds of things," he answered.

"Do you know if he has any books on soul travel?"

"I'm sure he does."

"Do you think your Dad would let me check out his library?"

"Sure."

I called his Dad as soon as I got back to work. He insisted I come by for, "a nice cup of soup before we see if I have the books you're looking for."

When I arrived, we had soup and interesting conversation. Then he took me into his library; the first books I noticed were the four I had been looking for, all lined up together on the shelf. He offered to loan them to me.

This is my definition of *synchronicity*.

Some of these stories are about serendipity. The word *serendipity* comes from the legend of the Three Princes of Serendip (Sri Lanka). These princes were committed to accomplishing wonderful things and always made complete and careful plans before setting out on their journeys of adventure. However, they never accomplished what they had set out to do; something always happened that made it impossible. But they always accomplished something wonderful; it just wasn't what they had planned.

The author John Barth, in his story, *The Last Voyage of Somebody the Sailor*, says it this way, "...you don't reach Serendib by plotting a course for it. You have to set out in good faith for elsewhere and lose your bearings... serendipitously."

This is an important part of the concept. Things don't just happen serendipitously. You have to have a plan; and then be willing to accept the unexpected, the unplanned event, be ready to *seize the moment*, before serendipity can play a role.

<hr/>

For years I was afraid to admit that difficult things often got done because of a lucky break. Somehow it didn't seem professional to share the fact that all of our wonderful plans wouldn't have been worth the paper they were printed on, if something unusual, unexpected, even miraculous hadn't happened.

Then, as the years passed and the products were shipped, and a record of accomplishment unequalled in the industry was achieved, it finally dawned on me that my ability to *seize the moment*, sense opportunity when she is only lightly scratching at the door, accept coincidence, synchronicity and serendipity into my plans (whenever they choose to make an appearance), was a major reason for my success as a producer, project manager, a leader of effective teams.

It doesn't always work out this way. Often it's just plain hard work. Once when we were trying to complete a game called

Murder on the Mississippi, the programmer, Adam Bellin, a sharp young guy with a big vision, had bitten off more than he could chew, and the product was in trouble. It was recommended I cancel the project and put Adam on something easier, "something he can handle." I didn't want to give up on the game or Adam. I liked the concept; we just needed to make it work.

Nothing unusual or unexpected happened to save us. It was just plain hard work. Ultimately all of the problems were solved, and *Murder on the Mississippi* shipped to great reviews, a product we could all be proud of.

So you can't depend on coincidence or luck; but that doesn't change the fact that if you're open to the possibility, something unusual, unexpected, even miraculous will often happen to make getting difficult things done much easier, even make it possible to accomplish the seemingly impossible. It's the opposite of Murphy's Law: Everything that can go wrong, will go wrong. I call it Fregger's Principle: Anything that can go right, will go right.

These small miracles can't happen if we don't give them a chance, if we're not open to whatever may occur, if we're not willing to accept coincidence and serendipity into our lives. This attitude is not something you turn on when the need arises. No, it's a lifestyle you embrace and practice daily. You learn to recognize opportunity in the smallest ways. You learn to *seize the moment* every chance you have!

I've enjoyed talking about *seizing the moment* and what a difference this practice can make in one's life experience. It's time to move on to the stories about creating the games that millions of you have played and are probably still playing. As you read these stories, think about the many different ways there are to *seize the moment*, and reflect on what a difference it makes when you decide to do just that.

Part One
ATARI

What A Ride! *Chapter 2*

Right from the first interview with Ron Berlin, VP of Personnel for Atari, I felt like I had come home. I'd always liked technology. I'd gotten my Master's Degree in Futuristics the year before (1980), and somehow that never fit in at Mervyn's where I was working. In fact, just before interviewing at Atari, I had purchased a new digital watch with a calculator on the face of it. My boss at Mervyn's didn't like it when I wore things that made me look like something other than a successful retailer. When he saw the watch, he took me aside.

"Brad, what is that gadget you're wearing on your wrist?"

"It's my new watch. The buttons are a calculator. Don't you like it?"

"Not really, it isn't professional. Couldn't you get something more acceptable?"

"I like this watch." He shrugged his shoulders and walked away. I felt bad, but I was determined to keep it.

A few weeks later I had my interview with Ron. The interview went great.

"I like you, Brad, and you seem to know what you're talking about. I'd like to offer you the Training Director position here at Atari. What do you say?"

"You've got yourself a Director of Training," I responded.

"Great. Can you start in two weeks?"

"Perfect. I can't wait."

"Okay, now I have one more question?" I looked at him expectantly. "Where did you get that great watch?"

Yep, I knew I had come home to Atari.

It was exciting to be part of the computer world, especially games, which I had always loved. But this wasn't my first experience with computers or computer games.

⚜

In the Spring of 1963, I was talking to my aunt, Joan Shogren, and she mentioned she had written a computer program based on artistic principles and was using it to create artworks with the San Jose State University computer. She called it "Computer Art." I got excited about the potential and talked her into doing a public showing. So on May 6, 1963, the first public exhibit of Computer Art in the world took place. The showing was very popular and was covered by the local San Jose paper. One of her pictures was chosen by the IBM Corporation as a mural to be placed on the side of one of its buildings in San Jose, California.

Later, I found myself between jobs and a friend of mine, Rod Geiman, president of a small company, Nutting & Associates, asked me if I would help him out. They were in the business of developing games for bars and arcades. Their games were alternatives to pinball: *Computer Quiz* and a new game called *Computer Space* were their big hits. Rod had a number of these products out in bars, arcades, laundromats, even the San Jose Airport...with no one to service them. Rod wanted me to help him out until he could find somebody to take the job. I said sure.

Computer Space was a hit; there were times when I got complaints the machine wouldn't work, only to discover the coin box was jammed full and the coins were backed up the shoot. *Computer Space* was the world's first commercial computer game. It was based on a popular game played on university computers throughout the United States, essentially two opponents in space ships fighting each other around a central sun, or gravity source. A young Nutting engineer, Nolan Bushnell, had programmed it. When he left Nutting, he did a simple game called *Pong* and started a company, Atari, and an entire industry.

Nutting & Associates closed down a couple of years later. The owner (not Rod) was more interested in evangelism. He built his own plane in his warehouse and flew off to save souls in Africa. It was his focus on evangelism that limited the success of *Computer Space*, not any lack of acceptance on the part of the playing public.

⚜

Now I was at Atari starting my second training department, preparing to develop the programs and hire the people needed to train the thousands of employees that Atari was hiring.

And I do mean thousands. In the two years I was at Atari we went from 3,500 employees to over 12,000; it was the fastest growing company in history. What a ride! I did more in those two years than the average Training Director for a Fortune 500 company does in ten years. Ron made it clear what he expected from me right from the start.

"Brad, we're bringing in a lot of green supervisors, people who aren't quite ready to take on the responsibility, but need to—right here and now. Your job is to train them as quickly as possible. While you're doing that, remember we're hiring thousands of people, people who need an orientation to Atari. Supervisory training and orientations, that's what I expect. Anything else you can do will be appreciated; anything else you do is up to you."

My marching orders were set, and I felt up to the task. Within four months I had hired four trainers and a secretary, put together a solid orientation program, and had begun putting my trainers through a "train-the-trainer" program. In addition, I had leased an outstanding training facility, the science building of a high school that had been recently closed. There was an amphitheater with seating for two hundred people, five classrooms, offices and a wonderful atrium that let the sun into the building itself. It was made for us. Before long we were doing orientations for hundreds of people a week. Everything was working like a well-oiled clock.

I decided to do a little survey of my own. I've always been a proponent of the Hewlett Packard philosophy of MBWA (Management by Walking Around). So I started wandering the halls of Atari, introducing myself and talking to numerous mid-level management people about their problems and concerns, trying to see if we might be able to help in some way.

With a company growing this fast, there were lots of problems. But I couldn't help noticing how committed the people were. In addition to learning about their needs, I was also affirmed that our orientation program was working. Often the person I was talking to would ask me if I had anything to do with the new employee orientation. When I modestly answered I had designed and implemented it, I was rewarded with extremely complimentary comments concerning the way their people were fitting in better and catching on faster since that program began. I have to give that single program all of the credit for the credibility our department gained at Atari. Our involvement in it opened many doors for me.

The needs were clear, and the first thing I discovered was that Ron was right again. After orientations, supervisory training was the greatest need the company had. I took the opportunity to tell those managers I met with about a Zenger Miller program I had used at Mervyn's with great success. Many wanted their supervisors to be in the first groups trained. Word got back to Ron that they couldn't wait for the supervisory training to begin. After that I had carte blanche to do whatever I wanted. There was no doubt my strategy of taking advantage of every opportunity, *seizing the moment* every chance I had, was paying off.

⟨ ⁓≈≋≋⁓ ⟩

One day, after I'd been at Atari about six months, Ron called me on the phone. "Can you come over? I want to introduce you to my new boss, Art Gemell."

"I'll be right there."

When I arrived Ron got up from his desk right way and led the way up to the senior executive offices on the second floor.

"Art arrived today, told me he had heard great things about you, and wanted to meet you as soon as possible." Ron said, as we climbed the stairs.

When we got to his office Art motioned us in and held out his hand in welcome. "Brad Fregger, great to meet you. Are you really as good as everyone has been telling me?"

"I don't know about that, but we have been able to accomplish quite a lot in the past few months. It's been great. I love it here and I hope you will too."

Art was a fairly big man, about my height, but I'm skinny and Art wasn't. He had dark hair and seemed very intelligent. He also seemed like he knew it. I could tell he was very personable, that he knew his way around in the corporate environment. He seemed very political. In a way, I think I envied that. From the beginning I'd never known how to play that game, and the lack of that skill had caused me problems more than once before.

"Well, I want to find out all about the programs you've been running and what else you have in mind. Could we have lunch tomorrow?" he asked.

"That's fine with me."

Lunch the next day went very well. We talked for quite awhile about his background, mine, what I was doing, and the kind of things he'd like to see done.

On the way back from lunch, as we were walking across

the parking lot back to the headquarters building, I spotted one of the recruiters, a young woman about twenty-two, whom I'll call Judy. I looked at Art and said, "Here comes one of the recruiters. Would you like to meet her?"

"Yes," he answered.

Judy was an attractive young lady with long blond hair and a perky appearance.

I waved to her and motioned her over. "Judy, I want you to meet Art Gemell. This is Ron's new boss. He just started yesterday."

She looked at Art with a kind of awe. Ron was Judy's boss's, boss's boss...this made Art pretty high up on the ladder.

Art put her at ease immediately, "Judy, tell me, what is it that you do in recruiting?" he asked.

"I specialize in support personnel, secretaries, clerks primarily?" she said quietly.

"That's very important work," Art responded. "We've got a lot to do here, and without enough support personnel...well, it will never get done. I'll tell you what, how many other recruiters are focusing on hiring support personnel?"

"There are two of us," she said.

"Here's the deal. At the end of the week, we'll total up the new hires for the two of you, and the one who has hired the most new people will get a weekend for two in San Francisco on me; hotel, meals, the works! How's that sound? he asked.

Judy thought the idea was great.

I was shocked. As an organizational professional, I couldn't begin to see how this could be positive in the long run. Art had no idea how the recruiting function was being run. The ultimate result would likely be a lowering of morale.

They talked for awhile longer, cementing the deal. When they were through, we continued our walk back.

"Did you notice the surprise on her face?" Art asked, obviously quite proud of himself.

I was still in shock, and before I knew it, I was saying, "She was definitely surprised. Do you think it was a good idea?"

"What do you mean? You saw the reaction," he asked in a "Do you know who the hell you're talking to?" tone of voice.

"What I mean is, the recruiting organization is working wonderfully, meeting all of it's goals and hiring good people, even under the pressures of this rapidly growing company. This could end up causing a morale problem," I responded. I could feel the passion rising. I could feel the automatic response mechanism I had when I judged that senior management was making a bad decision. I thought, "Oops, here I go again." But that didn't stop me.

"Did you stop to think about that?" I asked.

"Moi?" he said, sarcastically.

By this time we had reached the headquarters building and were climbing the staircase to the executive offices. He stopped on a landing and turned around, looking me directly in the eyes, and continued.

"Do you know anything about the French Middle Ages?" he asked.

"No," I said, wondering what this was all about.

"Well, let me educate you. Throughout France at this time were manors. Each of these manors had a Lord of the Manor. They were absolute monarchs of their domain. They could do anything they wanted...anything..."

He paused for a second, and it seemed to me he was thinking back to those times, to what it had been like to be Lord of the Manor. Then he said, "...including, have his pleasure with any single woman attached to the manor, anyone he wanted. Well, Brad, I'm Lord of the Manor, and don't you forget it."

He was saying this to intimidate me, to bring me down to size. What he didn't know was that I wasn't motivated by fear; I felt it, but I wasn't motivated by it.

Then he turned around and continued up the stairs. I followed. As we neared his office, I asked him, "Would you do the same kind of thing to the training department?"

He turned around as he reached his desk, looked at me, and said," Never, you're much too smart."

I very quickly proved just how stupid I was–I believed him.

Camelot *Chapter 3*

Soon Ron was gone. He and Art had never gotten along, Ron didn't trust him and Art knew this. Additionally, Art wanted someone of his own choice in charge of Corporate Personnel.

My new boss, Bob Kuntz, was hired in from the outside, one of the few positions not filled by personnel executives who had followed Art from his last place of employment.

Bob and I hit it off right away. We were both the kind of people who liked challenges, liked getting the job done. I was still having a great time. I was busy with all of the training that we were doing for the company. More and more members of management were inviting me to lunch and asking me to discuss a problem they thought might have a training solution.

Before I knew it, we had added communication skills, sales training, applicant interviewing, and team building to the slate of programs Atari people could choose. In every instance, these were programs management had asked for, programs designed to solve specific problems common throughout the organization. We even had a brochure, and I hadn't been at Atari a full year. In addition, I had introduced The Frank Lee Seminar to a select group of VP's who wanted to enhance their leadership potential.

I had found Frank when I was at Mervyn's. Actually he found me, called me on the phone and said, "When can I come over and tell you about my seminar?"

"How about we have lunch tomorrow?" I said.

At lunch he described the seminar for me. "It's a week long intensive for senior executives on leadership styles and team building. One of the great advantages is that they take it with peers from other organizations, including government. Discovering they share a lot of the same problems and challenges is very affirming and makes it easier for them to think about potential solutions. It's so much easier when you know you're not alone."

I loved the seminar and was convinced that it was just right for those executives that wanted to hone their leadership and team-building skills.

When that first Atari VP came to me for help for himself, I sent him off to Frank Lee. Atari very quickly became one of his best customers. I even had some director level executives attend, ones that were targeted for promotion.

⚜

One evening, I was at a big company dinner to celebrate the setting of some record or another (I lost track, there seemed to be so many of them). I ended up at a table with the Vice President of Strategic Planning.

"Well, Brad, how are things going over at Atari's Center for Training and Development?" he asked.

"Terrific!" I said. "It's everything I've ever dreamed of. You know what I like best about it?" I said.

"Tell me," he replied.

"It's the opportunity to give these young people working with me the experience of a lifetime. They're going to be talking about the time they spent at Atari for the rest of their lives." I said with pride in my voice.

He didn't say anything for a second or two, but I could see on his face that he was thinking back to a time of his own. Then he said, "When I was just getting started, I had a work experience like you're describing. It was wonderful; and you're right, I never have forgotten it. I wish I could have something like that again."

"You can," I said. "It's time now for us to create those environments for those that work in our areas. To move from being part of somebody else's Camelot to the creation of our own." I was challenging him to take responsibility, judging he wasn't giving back what he had earlier received.

"You don't know how much I'd love to be able to do that," he said. "But sometimes circumstances make it impossible."

I shrugged my shoulders and silently wrote him off as an ineffective executive that had risen beyond his competence. I wish I could apologize to him. Not for the way I acted, I didn't do anything wrong there; it was just a conversation between two executives, one that he probably doesn't even remember today. I would apologize for what I was thinking, the judgments I was making.

I soon discovered the hard way (it seems to be the only way I can learn anything) that there are times and circumstances you can't control.

As an effective executive, you can handle any problem, you can figure out some sort of working solution that will move you forward. There are even times when the most terrible problems, the greatest challenges, bring you and your group together as a team to be remembered, creating legends for the next generation. And, of course, there are those times when something happens, and a solution to a problem that had seemed to be unsolvable is dropped into your lap.

But there is one thing you can't conquer, one problem you can't overcome, a circumstance you can only live with, or walk away from. The VP of Strategic Planning was living with it; I ended up walking away. It's a boss, an owner, a president who is either determined you won't succeed, or is filled with an arrogant incompetence that destroys as quickly as it builds.

The choice is yours, live with it or walk away from it; you can't fight it. You're just wasting your efforts on a battle you will never win. Yes, sometimes *seizing the moment* means walking away.

⟨≈≋≋≋⟩

I never really fit in Art Gemell's organization. Like Ron, I didn't like him and I didn't trust him; and he was sharp enough to know that. Additionally, the culture he was creating called for us all to have nicknames, and I hate nicknames. I refused to answer to mine, and I refused to use the others'. It just wasn't working.

When Art began to effect the training organization negatively, stopping certain programs from happening, and transferring others out to the various divisional personnel executives, I went to see Bob.

"What's going on here?" I asked. "Aren't I doing a good enough job?"

"I don't know, Brad. I've thought and thought, and I can't figure out why Art is determined to destroy the finest training organization I have ever seen. What did you do to get him so mad at you?"

I thought back to that original conversation, to the judgments I made then and had continued to make. I had never been good at hiding my feelings. It was obvious what had happened.

"I think Art knows I don't like or trust him," I said. "It's hard to have an important executive in your organization that feels that way about you. I can see what's happened." I paused for a moment, considering my alternatives. "I don't think this is fixable. I can't change how I feel, and Art can't be expected to like it."

"What do you want to do?" he asked.

"I don't know, let me think about it."

It was time for me to go see one of my best friends, Don

Osborne. Don was the VP of Sales and Marketing for Atari CoinOp. He had been one of the most influential executives at Atari for years, the VP who had brought the world *Asteroids, Tempest, Centipede,* etc. We had grown up together, kids on the same block. Before even coming to Atari, Don and I had spent hours discussing plans for Atari CoinOp Events; we worked extremely well together. It was Don who had given Ron my resumé. Yep, it was time to go see Don.

"I'm sorry to hear that," Don said, after I had explained the whole thing to him. "You know, I'm looking for a VP of Sales; I've got to have some help. We'd have a terrific time together. What do you say?"

"That'd be great! I'd love it! We would have a terrific time together. We'll set the world on fire!"

"I think so, too!" he said. "You go back and talk to Bob, and I'll give Ray a call."

Bob liked the idea, too, and told me he'd give Art a call and let me know.

But, it wasn't to be. It turned out that it wasn't enough for Art that I would leave his organization; no, I had to leave Atari, to get out of his sight forever.

Don was devastated. Not only because we wouldn't be working together, but also because he thought he had more power than Art. It was a surprise to find out he didn't. I guess I wasn't surprised. Art really knew how to work the politics, and I'm sure he knew where all of the bodies were hidden. As far as I know, nobody ever went up against Art and won.

As it worked out, it was probably best that I left.

What Goes Up... Chapter 4

So the ride was over for me. It had been a thrilling one, a once in a lifetime opportunity; and I had seen it through to the end as far as I was concerned. From now on, whatever happened, the training at Atari would not be the same, would not have the same excitement, would not offer the same challenges. I had taken it from nothing in early 1981 to one of the greatest training departments in America in just eighteen months. I would always be proud of that.

What was I going to do now? It didn't take long to find out. Even before I left Atari, I had offers from Jack Zenger and Frank Lee. I was thinking of starting a training company to provide training services to other companies. Jack offered me the opportunity of handling some of their executive briefing sessions, and Frank wanted me to co-lead his seminars with him. It looked like I was going to be kept busy right from the start.

I also got an outstanding severance package. Bob was determined I be treated right. He felt Art was being extremely unfair, and he wanted to make it up to me. What I got amounted to four full months of salary. All that in addition to the immediate work that was waiting for me....

Chapter 4

The good-byes with my people were a little difficult, but the fact that they were so busy, and I was already involved in my new opportunities, made it easier than it might have been otherwise. It was still difficult to look around the Training and Development Center, knowing I would never see it again.

I ended up being on my own for a month. I did one executive briefing for Zenger Miller, and two seminars with Frank Lee.

It was at one of the Frank Lee seminars that I learned the power of process. Everything lead up to the final day, when Frank would lead a group session. The group would come up with a critical list of management objectives. This session determined the success of the seminar. The list had to reflect the week-long learnings. Frank never prepared for this session, never forced the responses. I was amazed.

"Frank, how can you trust that it will come out the way you want it to, the way you need it to?" I asked.

He looked at me, smiled, and said, "You have to trust the process. We spent a lot of time getting to this point; if we did it right (and I think we did) then the result will be right. That's how it works."

You have to trust the process. I've never forgotten those words. In truth, the list was slightly different for each group, but it was the right list for that group. The list was always a bit of a surprise, but it was always a pleasant one. Because the process was right in the beginning.

Trusting the process is *seizing the moment*. You've made your plans, done everything you can. And now you're committed to whatever happens, confident that things will work out just fine—however they work out.

Thinking about it now, I realize that we would have been modeling the wrong thing had we tried to force the list to fit our needs. What we were trying to show these executives was that true leaders often point people in a direction and then stand back and watch the action. True leaders are often surprised at what people accomplish when they are challenged and then given the freedom to reach the goals in their own way.

I've often been asked what went wrong at Atari, and I've read different opinions about why the company failed. There's a phrase I learned very early in my career that sums up what happened, "The fish stinks from the head."

The fact that Art Gemmel, the Senior Vice President of Corporate Administration, would have more power and influence than the Vice President of Sales and Marketing (actually acting President, since the Coin Op division was running without one at the time) of one of the most important divisions of the Atari Corporation, was one of the signs that Ray Kassar had his priorities screwed up.

Additionally, "oldtimers" were being poorly treated by the "professional management" that Ray was bringing into the company. Personnel was not the only division that lost a number of significant contributors in 1982. In fact, there wasn't a division in the company that wasn't affected. The end result was that there were too many executives who just didn't know what they were doing, didn't have a clue about the video game business.

Atari still might have made it through this difficult phase if it hadn't flooded the market with two terrible products, *ET* and *Raiders of the Lost Ark*. These two products alone brought down, not only Atari, but the entire video game industry.

First, Atari had insisted that their customers make their entire purchasing decisions for 1982 in the fall of 1981. This was a stupid decision. The products weren't even developed yet. How could retailers be expected to make intelligent buying decisions? Yet, Atari controlled eighty percent of the video game market, and these retailers were used to being caught short, were used to running out of product, with no chance of getting new shipments in time for the selling season. So, what did they do? They ordered heavy, without even knowing what they were ordering.

Atari, too, thought it didn't matter. If it came from Atari, people would buy it, would be happy with it. So senior management insisted that product be completed according to their schedule. They didn't care how long it took to design, develop and test a video game. They didn't want to know that it was a process that had to be treated with respect, one that had to be right, if you wanted the right outcome at the end.

The result was inevitable. The product that came out reflected the time and effort that went into it. It was bad product, unplayable product, product you told friends not to bother to buy.

❧

Not too long after I left Atari, Activison convinced me to come and work for them. When I arrived, one of the first things I was asked to do, was to put together a sales training program. Sales had begun to fall off, and they wanted to stop the trend before it got too far. I flew down to Southern California to join one of the sales people, Tom Johnson, making his rounds.

"You are not going to believe this," Tom said, as we drove into the parking lot of his first customer of the day, a small record store in East LA.

"Not going to believe what?" I asked.

"You'll see," he responded.

We walked into the store and he introduced me to the manager, "Bill, this is Brad Fregger from headquarters. He's the new training manager. He wants to see what it's like to sell video games these days. I think he'd like to see your back room."

"My pleasure. Come on, Brad, I think you'll enjoy this." Bill said.

Tom was right, it was hard to believe. In the backroom of this small record store was carton upon carton of *ET* and *Raiders* video games, hundreds of them.

"This is the problem, Brad," Tom said. "This chain has no open-to-buy for video games, not a penny to spend on new ones until they sell these; and they will never sell these, not even at a dollar each." Bill nodded in agreement.

"Why don't you send them back?" I asked.

"Atari won't take them back," Bill said. "We're stuck with them."

This scene was repeated time and time again as we continued Tom's sales calls for the day. It was very disheartening.

I went back to Activision and told them that all of the sales training in the world wasn't going to help. The market was flooded with bad product and, in my opinion, it would take more than a year to recover. Activision had to scramble just to survive.

No, don't believe all of the hype about a lack of quality product, a lack of competent game developers, or any one of the numerous reasons that have been given for Atari's demise. The truth is not complicated. In fact, it's very simple when viewed by an ex-retailer, who understands completely how retailers think.

Atari crashed and brought the entire video game industry down with it, because they flooded the market with two bad products, *ET* and *Raiders of the Lost Ark*, which resulted in no open-to-buy in that category. As far as most retailers were concerned, they never wanted to see another video game. It was three years before another company was able to break through their resistance and resurrect the video game market in the U.S. That company was Nintendo, and it took them two years to do it.

Ray Kassar was gone by mid-1983, but it was too late to save the company. It wasn't long before the lay-offs started and the company began to downsize. Just as they had been the fastest growing company in the world, now they were the fastest shrinking company; but at least they were still setting records.

Oh, I forgot to tell you, in addition to flooding the market with those two products, they ended up burying millions more in the desert. Yep, *ET* really can be found in the New Mexico desert, but it wasn't a flying saucer that crashed. It was Atari.

Part Two
ACTIVISION

The First Producers Chapter 5

When I began with Activision it looked like nothing could hold us back. While Atari still had the lion's share of the market, we were the premier outside supplier of video games for their 2600 game machine. With Atari beginning to push out inferior product, we were rapidly becoming the favorite supplier for those players who knew the difference. This was another fast growing company needing an effective training department; it wasn't like I hadn't done that before.

Activision's culture was entirely different from Atari's. Atari believed that sales and marketing was king and that the programmers were hired hands whose job it was to provide games the company could sell. It didn't matter what the games were or how good they were, "just get me some games...we'll figure out how to sell them."

Atari wouldn't even put the names of the programmers on the product. You never knew who programmed an Atari game. This was stupid. Talented, creative people need to be given credit for their accomplishments, their creations, as much or more than the rest of us. Atari was a Warner company. They were supposed to understand creative people.

Activision had been started by three software engineers, David Crane, Al Miller, and Bob Whitehead, who had left Atari for just that reason. At Activision the programmers were king. The games had to be fun to play and of high quality, nothing less was acceptable. The result of this attitude was that sales and marketing would blame it on the game if it didn't sell. Actually, it isn't that simple; there are lots of reasons why a game (or book, record, movie, etc.) doesn't sell. Sometimes the reasons are beyond anyone's control.

At Activision my boss was Ken Coleman, an outstanding personnel executive who had come from Hewlett Packard. He'd heard about me from one of his staff, Mary Costa, who I had worked with at Mervyn's. Mary and I had become very good friends, and when she heard I had left Atari, she told Ken he had to get me.

I wasn't an easy sell. I was already making very good money, and I hadn't been on my own for a month yet. But I did have a weak spot. My son, Jon, had just started college, and we were concerned about the insecurity of having our own business.

Additionally, Ken was good at stroking my ego, "Brad, we are one of the fastest growing companies in America, and we are going to be one of the most successful. You are looking at some great bonuses and very nice stock options. We only hire the best there is, and we think you're the best training guy around. That's why we want you."

His arguments were compelling and I accepted the job.

Ken was one of the finest executives I ever worked for. Right from the beginning he stimulated me in ways that no one ever had before. And most importantly, I quickly developed a high respect for him as both a person and a professional. Working with Ron, and then Bob, at Atari was great because they left me completely alone. While Ken essentially trusted me to do what needed to be done, he was quick to spot a flaw in a program or design. In addition, he had high integrity and knew the difference between right and wrong.

It was very important to Ken that decisions be made for

the right reasons, and that if we had to make an unpopular decision, we would examine every alternative before making it. This was a change I welcomed.

***

Within six months after I began at Activision, early in 1983, Atari shipped *ET* and *Raiders*, and the end of the video game business was at hand. Our sales fell off so significantly that it became necessary to instigate a major lay-off. This meant we had to put together an effective outplacement program immediately. I have never seen a difficult situation handled so well, an example of how Activision cared for it's people. Ken was a master at this sort of thing, and if it's possible to lay off a lot of people in the right way, we handled it better than any company I have ever seen before or since.

This was a major layoff in a highly visible industry, locally second only to the layoffs Atari had just begun. This was front-page news; we had reporters, TV cameras, the works. As usual they were looking for bad news, but all that made the six o'clock news was, "I love Activision, I hate to be leaving, to be one of the ones who has to go. But, it's not their fault, and they're treating me very well. I wish them all the luck in the world." We felt great!

We were able to place every single person who took advantage of our outplacement program. It was a phenomenal success. The only thing we hadn't planned for was the guilt that was felt by those that stayed. Healing the survivors turned out to be our biggest challenge. It hadn't dawned on us that the ones left behind might need help too.

***

This was when Activision first tried to make the switch from a video game company to a computer game company.

There was a dramatic difference between the two in the eyes of the distributors and retailers, not to mention the customer. We never quite internalized that. To Activision, it was all the same thing; the only difference was you had more memory to work with. The Atari game machine had a maximum of 8K of memory, while the Atari 800 and Commodore 64 had 64K. We figured we would just do better games and people would pound down our doors.

We didn't see any reason why this couldn't happen. We had some of the best computer games engineer/designers in the world, and our products continued to receive rave reviews. There was a high degree of optimism in regards to our future and the future of computer games.

However, when we looked at the management of our product development effort, we felt something was missing, a level of professionalism and expertise that didn't match what we had in engineering. Remember, this was very early in the computer games industry. It was impossible to go out and find somebody with experience in the field.

Companies were bringing in project managers to oversee the development of the games, in much the same way that applications and systems companies used project managers to oversee the development of their software. Activision had done the same thing.

It finally dawned on us that we weren't in the applications and systems business. We were in the entertainment business. The model wasn't right for us and probably negatively impacted our ability to consistently produce high quality game software. Senior management decided it needed to create a model based on the entertainment industry. The decision was made to move from project managers to producers. As far as I know, Activision was the first company to use producers to manage the software development cycle.

Typically a project manager was responsible for the completion of the project on time and on budget, acting as a liaison between the software engineers and management. He was supposed to keep pressure off of the engineers so they wouldn't be hampered as they worked to complete their projects. But he had very little responsibility for the product itself. Activision believed it was important to have someone in charge who would also take some responsibility for the product, its design, development, even interface with marketing. This is what the producer would do.

We were concerned that we find just the right person to be our first producer. We had three product managers, but it was perceived that they wouldn't be accepted as producers by the engineers. Remember, Activision had been formed by three software engineers. At Activision, engineers were king. To be effective, producers needed to gain control, prove their worth. It would be an uphill battle for anyone, but probably impossible for those who had already been accepted as project managers.

Where do we find somebody like this? As I said, nobody existed with this type of experience. What we did was put together a list of characteristics and skills that we thought would be important in an individual assigned this responsibility. Then we began to look for people who matched this list. After a year and a half, we still hadn't found anyone.

At about this time I was flying back to San Jose from a meeting in Los Angeles, and I had taken out the list one more time to see if I might get some inspiration. As I read down the list of characteristics, I began to recognize the person the list described. The more I thought about it, the more it seemed as if the list was describing me. Was it possible that I could be Activision's first producer? Why not? I decided to take a chance, *seize the moment*.

When I got back to Activision, I went in to see Ken and I said, "I think I've found our first computer games producer."

Ken had been busy writing at his desk, but with this statement he looked up quickly and said, "You have?"

"I think so. He seems to have all of the characteristics we've been looking for."

"Who is it? Do I know him?" he asked.

"You know him pretty well," I said.

"Well, who is it?"

"Me."

That stopped him. He just looked at me for a minute; he didn't say anything. Then, "I'll talk to you about it tomorrow."

I left, not knowing what had gone on in his mind. The next day he called and asked me to come to his office.

When I got there, he got up from his desk, came around to meet me, and said, "I talked with Tom Lopez (Activision's Vice President of Editorial Development) and we agree with your assessment. Congratulations, you're our first computer games producer. You start in a week."

I was flabbergasted. I didn't really believe anything would come of my suggestion. Now, in just one week, I'd have a completely new job, producing computer games...what had I gotten myself into?

With my move to the Editorial Development department, the three product managers were also made producers. There was no way we could do anything else and, to tell the truth, they deserved it. They worked hard and were effective. They, too, needed the opportunity to prove themselves in this way.

However, the bulk of responsibility for making it work was with me and to make that very clear, I was made the producer for all products designed and programmed by the founding engineers.

At this time, our hottest new product was *Pitfall II* by David Crane. David was the best known video games designer in the world, and *Pitfall II* was the sequel to *Pitfall*, one of the top video games of that time. Activision had high expectations for it. The market had softened up a little and we were able to get some product on the shelves. We believed that with *Pitfall II* we had the chance to bring the video game business back to its previous level of success.

Since David was one of our founding engineers, I was his

new producer, and the first thing I did was to take a trip to New York with my new boss, Tom Lopez, to do a press tour for *Pitfall II*. I don't even remember the tour, only how nervous I was.

Probably the one thing that gets most in the way of *seizing the moment* is nervousness, a fear of screwing up, making a fool of yourself. At times like this you are so focused on surviving that you can't even think about the moment, let alone seize it. This happened to me on that first trip with Tom. It was a time when I was determined to make a good impression, to convince him that he had made the right decision when he selected me to be a member of his staff.

The first night we were there we had dinner in one of Tom's favorite restaurants, a very high class Italian place around 56th Street, or Avenue, I don't know, my mind was in a fog. At the dinner was Tom, Jim, the producer who managed products for our New Jersey Design Center, and the woman, I'll call her Amy, who handled our public relations in New York City. Everyone except me seemed right at home. I'd never even seen the inside of a restaurant this elegant before. I was used to eating at fast-food places. A terrific night out meant dinner at Tony Roma's. (It still does!)

I remember clearly excusing myself to go to the bathroom and then, while I was standing at the urinal, deciding what I would order, so I wouldn't have to hesitate, look stupid, while everyone waited for me. I knew this place must have *fettuccini alfredo*, that would be my main course. And since they were an Italian restaurant, everyone would probably have wine. What kind should I order? This was a problem, both red and white wines gave me a headache, "I know, I'll order *rosé*." I went back to the table confident I wouldn't make a fool of myself.

The waiter came to take our orders, and I was so busy focusing on what I had just decided that I didn't hear what the others ordered. Finally it was my turn.

"And you, sir, what will you have?" he asked me.

He was tall, stately, with slick black hair and a manner

about him that demanded no nonsense.

"I'd like the *fettuccini alfredo* and some of your *rosé* wine," I responded.

Everything stopped. There was complete silence throughout the entire restaurant. All eyes turned toward me. I have never seen such looks of disbelief in my life. I looked toward Tom...no help there...toward Jim...no help there...toward Amy...no help there either. I looked up at the waiter, a questioning look on my face...what had I done wrong?

He looked back with a look of disgust that I had never seen before or since. It was as if I was the lowest of lowest scum on the face of the Earth. He seemed to savor the moment, savor my embarrassment, as if determined that I should suffer as much as possible. Finally, he said, "We don't serve *rosé* wine, sir." His pronunciation of "sir," the tone of voice, the inflection, was used as an insult.

Now what do I do? I had planned on *rosé*. I didn't have a second choice. I thought as quickly as I could, but my mind was made of molasses and I drew a blank. Finally, "Could I have a glass of water?"

"Wahter...you want plain wahter?" he said with contempt.

"You do have water, don't you?" I asked.

And with that he turned on his heel and left.

I looked back at Amy and asked, "What did I do that was so wrong?"

"Let me put it this way," she said, "...if you were my date, and you ordered *rosé* wine in this restaurant, I would have excused myself to go to the bathroom, and I would have never returned."

My worst fears had been realized. My ignorance when it came to matters like this had been broadcast to the entire restaurant. I was sure Tom was deciding he had made a big mistake, that I would never succeed as a producer. And it wasn't over yet.

In a few minutes the waiter was back with a glass of plain water, "Your wahter, sir." And then he proceeded to give a beer to each of the others.

After he left I said, "I didn't know I could have beer."

Amy quickly jumped in, "Oh, would you like a beer? Waiter! Waiter!" she hollered across the restaurant.

He came back, and I saw a glint of amusement in his eyes. Then he said, "Yes," in his deep professional voice.

I looked at Amy and saw the same amusement in her's, and I knew they were playing with me. The problem was, I couldn't do anything about it. I was stuck and had to live through it as best I could.

"He's decided that he would like a beer. Could you bring one please?" she asked.

"Of course," and he left, but was soon back with my beer, as well as the hors d'oeuvres the others had ordered. I would have loved to have had some of the shrimp that Tom had, but I wasn't stupid enough to mention that out loud.

After hors d'oeuvres, the waiter brought the others their salads, and I realized that this was one of those places where you had to order your entire meal, that when you ordered a main course, you got the main course and that was all. I awkwardly waited, sipping my beer as the others finished their salads.

Finally, it was time for the main course, and the waiter brought me the smallest helping of *fettuccini alfredo* I had ever seen.

I did get some cheesecake for dessert, but this was not a good beginning to my new career as a computer games producer.

This was without a doubt one of the most embarrassing evenings of my life, one of the few times I wasn't able to *seize the moment* and run with it.

The World's Greatest Easter Egg   *Chapter 6*

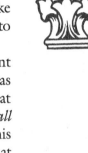

When I got back from New York, the first order of business was to develop the Atari 800 and Commodore 64 versions of *Pitfall II*. Mike and Tim were the two programmers assigned to the task.

David had packed a tremendous amount of playability into the original version; it was unbelievable when you stop to consider what little computer memory it actually took. *Pitfall II* was Activision's first 8K video game. This was twice the size of any other video game that had been developed for the Atari 2600, but it was still only 8K. Now we were doing the exact same game for two new computers, each of which had 64K available. What were we going to do with all that extra memory?

The way I tend to operate as a producer is to get everyone involved in discussions relating to design and development. So, I sat down with Tim and Mike to plan how we would upgrade the *Pitfall II* video game to a computer game.

It was obvious from the beginning of the discussion that these guys had two very different opinions as to how the extra memory should be spent. Tim wanted to take advantage of the C64's superior graphics capability to make the game more beautiful, create a stunning product. While Mike didn't have the graphics capability of the C64 and, therefore, wasn't interested in trying to make the game prettier, he wanted to create an entire second level that would be as challenging as the game itself, maybe even more challenging.

I can only blame my inexperience for the decision I ended up making; let each of them do what they wanted. Tim made the C64 more beautiful, a stunning computer game that reviewers and players alike loved. And Mike created an entire new level that was both bigger and better than the original game. In Mike's version, after you completed the first level (essentially the original game), you entered a new series of caverns with new places to explore, all new challenges, and a puzzle to solve.

It was during development of *Pitfall II* for the Atari that I learned how programmers will often set goals for themselves that are almost impossible to attain. When you're doing a game, you're almost always on a tight schedule. The schedule would have been tight if Mike had just converted the original game, leaving it almost exactly the same. Now, he had committed to adding all that additional game play, and still completing it on time. As a result, for the last two months of the project, Mike ended up working twenty hours a day for seven days a week. He actually brought in a mattress so he could grab a few hours of sleep without having to go home. It almost killed him, and I mean that literally. He got very sick, and I vowed never to let that happen again.

I still see companies that brag about how many hours their people are putting in, how they invent ways to stay at the office, bringing in sleeping bags, ordering in pizza at 3:00 am, etc. This is ludicrous, and doesn't really buy you anything. You think you are getting all this extra commitment, but it doesn't work that way. "There's no such thing as a free lunch." Ultimately, somebody will pay for all of those extra hours in heavy crunch mode, and just as often as not, it will be the company that pays, not the employee.

There was also an unexpected pleasant development. I was able to renew a friendship and at the same time create a new relationship that would serve me well over the next few years. It turned out we needed some music for the surprise ending of Mike's new level. To accomplish this, I called on an old friend from my Mervyn's days, Ed Bogas. Ed is one of the finest musicians in the world, and one of the most successful in the San Francisco Bay Area. I had originally met Ed when he was just getting started in his own business. I was doing a "Scarf Demo" video tape for Mervyn's; and Joe Vesce, my boss, thought since this tape would be played in all of Mervyn's stores, would be seen by thousands of customers, it would be a good idea if I had some professional help. Ed was truly that and more. Over the years we became very good friends, and I often called on him when I needed music for a game or a demo. Ed's name may not be familiar, but his music probably is, especially if you saw the *Garfield the Cat* TV shows.

It was a tough development schedule, but we completed the projects on time, and I turned them over to marketing. When I handed them to the marketing manager, I said, "Here they are, final versions of *Pitfall II* on the C64 and the Atari 800!" I was real proud of our accomplishment.

"That's great! Anything special I should know as I put together the final marketing plans?" he asked.

"Only that they aren't exactly the same," I said.

"What do you mean?" he asked.

"Well, the Atari version has a completely new level attached, with a bunch more game play. We couldn't do that with the C64, so we upgraded the C64's graphics."

"I don't understand," he sounded confused. So I explained what we had done.

"But that won't work!" he exclaimed.

"Why not?" I asked.

"Our marketing plan depends upon promoting these two products concurrently, using the same advertising and public relations. How can we advertise the new features when they aren't available in both products. The C64 customer is going to feel cheated. This is terrible!" He was not happy.

As I thought it over, I realized I had made a big mistake. It was wrong to allow these two products to take such entirely different paths. An experienced producer would have seen this, would have anticipated the marketing issues. I had failed in my responsibility as a producer. Sure, I got the products done, on time and on budget, but my job demanded much more than that.

I was told to take the extra game out of the Atari 800 version. All that work gone to waste. I went back to Mike with the bad news.

There's a phrase in computer software that grabs the imagination, *Easter Egg*. An Easter Egg is an added feature, or "programmer joke" that can only be accessed through a secret series of commands that, theoretically, only the programmer knows. Often the programmer will "leak" the information needed to get to the Easter Egg, because he (or she) wants the public to know about it, is only trying to keep it from the publisher.

One of the best examples of an Easter Egg involved my brother-in-law, Barry Pearsall. Barry did the programming for the first digital watch. He was with National Semi-Conductor at the time. While doing the code, he thought it would be neat to add something very personal, so he made it so the watch alarm would go off at a random time on his birthday. Of course, the manufacturer was not aware of this, nor the customers. If you had one of those first digital watches, and you noticed that it went off suddenly when you hadn't set it…that's an Easter Egg.

When push came to shove, I couldn't waste the time or the effort that was put in, couldn't cheat the customer out of these wonderful enhancements to *Pitfall II*, and, most important of all, I couldn't disappoint Mike. So that is how *Pitfall II* on the Atari 800 had the most extensive Easter Egg in the history of computer games, an Easter Egg that was bigger and better than the original game.

I didn't tell anyone I had decided to keep the new level in as an Easter Egg, and it didn't come to anyone's attention until technical support got a couple of calls from C64 customers who wanted to know how to get to the additional level on their machine. When tech support called me, I didn't know what they were talking about. And I was ***much*** too busy to research the issue.

I Love This Movie...
Let's Do the Game! Chapter 7

Tom Lopez left and two things happened in quick succession. First, the department name was changed to Product Development, and second, the new Vice President of Product Development was Dick Lehrberg. Dick had been with Sears before coming to Activision. Now he was in charge of product development for one of the top game companies in the world.

If there's anything that computer game developers like almost as much as their games, it's a good movie. Sometimes, we would take off in the middle of the afternoon to go see the latest film, especially if it had a science fiction or fantasy theme. That's why we were all at the first matinee performance of *Ghostbusters*.

Ghostbusters had everything; we knew from the first scene that we were watching a film destined to become a classic. Afterwards, we went to the pizza parlor and talked about how much we loved it. Then somebody said, "It would make a great game!"

We all agreed, and then David Crane said, "If it's still available, I'm going to do it."

This was an interesting development. Usually the rights to a movie like *Ghostbusters* are sold well before the movie is made. In this way, the game can be released at about the same time the movie comes out. Here David was talking about licensing the rights to do a computer game for a movie that had already been released. Even if we were able to secure the rights, the development schedule would be challenging to say the least.

David got what he wanted. Within a week Activision had secured the video and computer game rights to *Ghostbusters*, and I found myself up against David's preconceived ideas as to the role of a project manager—even if he was called a producer. David put the team together, designed the game, and managed the process. He pretty much asked me to stay out of his way. In his eyes, I had no credibility, could offer nothing to the project, except to act as his assistant and keep management off his back.

Then, about half way through the project, he came to me and said, "I have to take a month off; I don't have any choice. Adam is doing fine, but you will need to manage things until I get back." He didn't sound like he had much confidence things would work out.

"You do what you need to do. I'll take care of things here." I was actually glad this was happening. I knew the team David had put together was up to the task, but they were also young and inexperienced and needed direction. This was my chance to prove to David that my involvement as producer would be a good thing. If I convinced David, everything else would fall into place.

The assistant programmer on the project was Adam Bellin. Adam was fast and good, but he needed help in knowing what to do when, and in knowing what direction to take when things weren't working out quite right. I was able to provide the direction he needed, and we accomplished more in one month than we would have even if David had been there. We also had to make some changes to the game play; there were problems that we discovered once we got it playing. I was confident David would approve of our changes.

When he returned, Adam and I sat him down and showed him what we had accomplished in his absence. He had come to the meeting with trepidation. There were those in senior management who had been angry with his taking time off during this critical phase of the project, and he personally had felt guilty about it.

About half way through the presentation, he looked at me and I saw relief in his eyes. Then he said, "You guys have done a terrific job. I couldn't have done it better myself. Maybe I should go to Hawaii more often."

It was a high compliment, paid by the best in the industry. Adam and I were very proud of what we had accomplished.

I had taken advantage of this opportunity to gain David's acceptance, knowing how important this was to my long-term success as a producer at Activision. I had accomplished this, but then David surprised me.

At Activision the stars were the game developers, the engineers. This was David Crane's *Ghostbusters*, he was the one who got the credit, just like in the movies. This was how it should be, but David went further and in doing so gave me the compliment of my life. He insisted my name go on the package as the producer. He told me, "You deserve the credit, Brad. Without you, we never would have made it." I was elated. This had never happened before. Never had a producer been given credit on the package of a product. When I saw the final package...well, what a thrill to see your name exposed like this, for the world to see for the first time.

But it wasn't to happen. When the other producers found out, they complained bitterly. At product development management meetings during the first half of the project, I had mentioned the problems I was having with David, how I was not being involved in any of the decisions and how frustrating it was. Then when things changed, I didn't bother to tell them; I had just gotten to work. Now I had my name on the package, and they couldn't see what I had done to deserve that. They had been doing this kind of work for much longer than I had and didn't feel it was fair.

Dick agreed with them and tried to help me see how it really wasn't fair for me to be singled out. It didn't do any good. I went ballistic. When I look back on it now, I am embarrassed and saddened by how I acted, by the problems I caused Dick over this situation. I went to every executive in the company and screamed bloody murder about how I was being taken advantage of. I told everyone how hard I had worked, how David had seen that and personally sought to reward me in this way, and yet a couple of jealous peers were stopping it from happening...it wasn't fair.

I was such a jerk. I should have been given a corrective interview, but I wasn't even talked to. This was one more example of how my passion can serve me poorly, can result in actions and reactions that I am ashamed of for the rest of my life. All of the energy was completely wasted and probably cemented my reputation as a passionate, uncontrollable individual, someone you want around if you're in trouble, but one hell of a difficult guy to manage.

The package, of course, went out without my name as producer.

Dick has since told me that, in retrospect, he probably made the wrong decision at that time. He had not been aware of my actual contribution to the project and listened too much to the other producers' concerns and not enough to what really happened. He did make it up to me, though.

The next movie we did a computer game version of was *Aliens*. This was another terrific team effort, an unbelievable accomplishment, from start to finish in three months. When I think about the creative environment that existed in the in-house development lab at Activision at this time, the products we produced, what we were able to accomplish, it's truly mind-blowing. Most people never have an experience like this, and I was having my second. First Atari, and now this. God, was I blessed!

And when the package came out, designed like a movie poster, there was my name—Produced by Brad Fregger—I have to admit, it felt real good.

Seizing the Moment

Chapter 8

Once in a great while you get the perfect opportunity to tell the perfect joke, to *seize the moment* in this way. Those of us who care about such things wait a lifetime for these chances and then milk them to their maximum.

My dad, who lives for these kinds of opportunities, waited his entire life to have dinner with someone named Royce. There needed to be a number of people present and a very special item on the menu.

When the time came, he didn't hesitate. In a loud clear voice he said, "Would you please pass the rolls, Royce?" Everyone broke up and wonder of wonders, Royce had never had that happen to him before.

About fourteen years ago a group of us from Activision were attending the Consumer Electronics Show in Chicago. About fifteen of us were out to dinner together and the conversation got around to Dick Lehrberg and the fact that he seemed to know everyone in the industry.

This was hardly an exaggeration. Dick really did seem to know everyone—other publishers, software developers, retailers, distributors; it didn't matter, if you worked in the industry, you probably knew Dick.

Let me set the scene for you. We were all sitting around one big table in this classy Chicago deep dish pizza restaurant. I was near one end and Dick was near the other.

I waited for a slight pause in the dinner conversation and then said in a loud clear voice, "You don't know the half of it!"

I had everyone's attention and I stood up to tell my story.

"Last year Dick and I were walking past the Fairmont Hotel in San Francisco, and we got into this conversation. I decided to have some fun with him, so I said, 'Dick, everyone says you know everyone, but you don't. For example, you don't know him,' and I pointed at the doorman.

"At just that moment the doorman noticed us, waved and hollered, 'Hello, Mr. Lehrberg!'"

Believing the joke ended up being on me, the dinner party broke out in spontaneous laughter.

I waited for it to quiet down and then continued, "This was obviously a coincidence, so I said, 'You don't know her,' and I pointed at a woman leaving the Fairmont garage in her car. Just then she noticed us, waved and hollered, 'Hi Dick!'"

Again my audience broke out in delighted laughter.

After a moment, I said, "It turned out Dick had done a conference in that hotel, and I had coincidentally pointed out the woman who had coordinated it for him.

"Coincidence or not, this was frustrating me. So I decided to end it right there.

"'Well, you don't know Frank Sinatra...' and this guy..."

I pointed down to the end of the table where Dick was sitting.

"...had the gall to suggest that he did know Frank, that he had met him during a special promotion when he was a merchandise manager for Sears."

They didn't laugh this time. Some of them turned to

Dick and silently asked, using body language and expression, "Is this true?" Dick looked embarrassed. He wasn't saying anything.

"'No way,' I said. 'You may have been introduced, but he would never recognize you on the street.' Dick shrugged his shoulders, so I decided to challenge him. 'I'll tell you what, the rat pack is in Vegas. Let's fly down there this weekend. We'll go to the show. If Frank recognizes you, I pay for the trip. If not, you pay.' I knew he'd have a good reason for not taking me up on my offer.

"'Okay, it's your money,' he said.

"Well, we get to Vegas and the first thing we do is go to the hotel to get tickets for the show. But the line is around the block. I suggest we go to the front of the line and check out the situation.

"We get up to the front where the manager notices us and comes right over. I'm afraid he's going to ask us to get to the back of the line. Instead, he says, 'Dick, good to see you. What are you doing here?'

The laughter had quieted down. This was becoming awesome. They couldn't believe what they were hearing, but they knew it must be true.

"'We were hoping to see Frank, what's our chances?'

"'Excellent. I just had a cancellation...front row, center for the next show...want'em?'

"You bet we did and within minutes we were seated ringside waiting for the show to begin."

I paused to take a drink and shook my head. Then I looked up and around the table, making eye-contact with everyone, including Dick, and said, "You won't believe what happened next..."

"Frank comes out on stage for a quick, let's get acquainted before the show begins...looks down...and sees Dick...stops what he's saying in mid-sentence and says, 'Dick...good to see you! Ladies and gentlemen, an old friend, a great guy, Dick Lehrberg....enjoy the show...come back stage to say hello when it's over.'

"I was out one trip to Vegas."

My audience, almost as a single person, turned with something like awe and looked at Dick, believing the story was over. Wrong!

I sighed deeply, waited for this to sink in, and then I said, "Most of you know me pretty well. You know I don't give up easily. Well, I was determined to mention someone who Dick would have no chance of knowing...I had to find someone. Then I had it! He was Jewish. I turned to him and said, 'You don't know the Pope...so there!'"

Again, they all burst out in laughter, glad to have this chance for a release of the tension that had been building.

"You think this is funny...but this guy told me that he knew the Pope!" I exclaimed in frustration. "I had to call his bluff."

Again there was total silence, again I had their complete attention.

"I told him, 'You're crazy...this time you're bluffing. I'll tell you what...same deal. We go to Italy, we'll take our wives. If you know the Pope, if he recognizes you, I'll pay all expenses. If not, you pay.' There was no way he was going to accept this bet.

"'It's your money,' Dick shrugged.

"About a month later we were in Italy. While our wives were out shopping, Dick and I were waiting in the plaza where the Pope gives his blessing...what's the name?...I can never remember it..."

I acted confused, frustrated. Someone in the group spoke up, "Saint Peter's Square."

"That's it, thank you...well, we had arrived very early to be sure we were in the right spot so the Pope could see us. But as the time approached we got pushed further and further back. Finally, Dick said, 'Tell you what. You stay here. I'll go see the Pope and then appear on the balcony with him. Then you'll know that I know him.'

"'If you don't appear on the balcony, I win. Right?'

"'Right.'

"I figure I've got this one won.

"The problem was, I kept getting pushed further and further back; and when two people appeared on the balcony, I couldn't tell who they were. There was a guy next to me with a pair of binoculars, so I asked him, 'Do you know who that is up on the balcony?'

"'I don'ta know the guy with'a the red'a robes, but the guy next to him, that'sa Dick Lehrberg!'"

And I sat down.

For a moment nobody said anything, and then it began to dawn on them that I had taken them for a long ride. And the laughter began.

I'd waited years for just the right time to tell that joke. When the *moment* came...I *seized* it.

Medical Interlude

One Friday evening in September of 1984, I was working a bit late with Ed Bogas finishing up some music for one of our games. When we finished working, I found I didn't even have the energy to carry my computer down to the car, so I asked Ed if he'd carry it down for me.

"Aren't you feeling well, Brad?"

"Awful weak. The doctor said this might happen. I'm taking some new medicine."

I had had a chronic cough for about four months that I was getting tired of putting up with, so I had gone to see a doctor who specialized in such things. After a battery of tests, he concluded I had asthma and prescribed some medicine he thought would help.

"Don't be surprised if you begin to feel weak. That's a common symptom of this condition," he told me.

Within twenty-four hours of taking the new medication, I began to feel *very* weak. The weakness was so bad that when I got home that night, I had to lay down and rest for awhile after I walked in from the car. Still, the doctor had said this might happen, so I wasn't too worried.

My mother was staying with us at the time, because my father was in the hospital recovering from a heart operation; he had a new heart valve installed. During dinner we began to discuss who would be visiting my dad that night. I said I felt kind of tired and maybe I wouldn't go.

"I'm worried about you," my mother said. "I'm afraid there might be something seriously wrong with you."

"The doctor explained that I might begin to feel tired," I replied. "I'm sure this will pass."

"I wouldn't assume that," she said. "Have you had any other symptoms?"

"Actually, I have noticed that my stools are very dark. The doctor did say that there might be other symptoms besides the weakness."

"You know, Brad, those symptoms are the same as the symptoms for a bleeding ulcer and massive blood loss. Maybe you should go and have it checked."

"But the last time I had an ulcer I had lots of pain, and this time I am experiencing no pain at all."

"Sometimes there is no pain; that's called a silent ulcer. What harm would there be in going to the clinic and having it checked out?" she responded. "At least call your doctor."

So I called the doctor and told him what was going on.

"I'm sure it's only a drug reaction. If you feel better having somebody check it out, go down to the urgent care facility and have the doctor on duty take a look at it."

After I hung up the phone, we decided that I would drive down to the clinic while Kathie and my mother would go visit my dad. Then we would meet back at the house.

When I entered the clinic, the first thing they did was take my blood pressure. Then they asked me to lie down, and they took my blood pressure again. Then they asked me to stand up, and they took my blood pressure a third time. Then they took some of my blood.

A short time later the doctor came into the examining room and he took my blood pressure, laying down and standing up. Then he shook his head and walked out of the room.

The examining room was next to his office and, since he

left my door open, I could hear him make a phone call.

"Dr. Johnson, this is Dr. Smith at the Urgent Care Facility." *Pause.* "But..." *Pause.* "But, Dr. Johnson, you are listed here as the doctor on call tonight." *Pause.* "I'm sorry, sir, I won't bother you again."

There was a longer pause, and then I heard, "Hello, Dr. Robbins, this is Dr. Smith at the Urgent Care Facility, and I wonder if you could help me out?" *Pause.* "I know, sir, that you are not on call, but the doctor who I thought was on call says that he is not, and I really need to consult with someone about this case." *Pause.* "I'm sorry, sir, to have bothered you. I won't bother you again."

I heard him hang up the phone, then a deep sigh, and then the chair being pushed out. A few seconds later he was at my door.

"Is there something I can help you with?" I asked.

He looked kind of surprised that I would be asking him that question, and then he said,

"It's just that your symptoms are confusing me."

"Well, maybe talking it over with me will help you understand what's going on." I responded.

He looked at me for a couple of seconds and then said, "The results of your blood pressure readings lead us to believe you have had a massive loss of blood. But the results of the blood analysis seem to say that isn't true, and I don't know what to believe."

"What about the blood analysis makes you believe I haven't lost a lot of blood?" I asked.

"Your white blood cell count is normal. Normally, after a massive loss of blood, the white blood cell count is up significantly."

"Could it be that I have lost the blood so quickly and so recently that the white blood cell count has not had a chance to rise yet?" I asked.

"That could be it," he said.

He turned around and went back to his office, and I decided it was time to give Kathie a call.

I got up from the examining table and walked down the hall, looking for a phone I could use.

"What are you doing?" the first nurse I saw hollered at me.

"Looking for a phone," I answered.

"You can't be walking around," she said. "Sit down right there in that chair, and I'll get you a wheelchair."

When Kathie answered I said to her, "It looks like the chances that they're going to let me drive home are not very good. Could you have Mom drive you over here?"

"Sure, I'll be right over," she answered.

"Might plan on a long night. My guess is we'll end up at the hospital," I told her.

"Okay," and she hung up.

After calling Kathie I went back to the examining room and got back up on the table. Dr. Smith came in, "I've thought about what you said, and I think you should go over to the hospital. How did you get here?"

"I drove," I answered.

"You can't drive to the hospital. Can somebody come and get you, or should we call an ambulance?"

"My wife is on her way over," I said. "I just called her."

"Good. Now when you get to the hospital, they are going to want to put a tube down your throat to try and find out what is going on down there."

"No way they're going to put a tube down my throat," I responded.

"They need to, if they are going to be able to help you," he said.

"Don't get me wrong," I said. "I'm not against it. It's just that the last time I had a major illness the doctors and nurses tried for hours to put a tube down my throat, and they never were able to get it down."

"Well, we'll see.... In the meantime, I'll make arrangements for a doctor to meet you there." And I heard him go back into his office to make another call.

"Dr. Thomas?" *Pause.* "This is Dr. Smith at the Urgent Care Facility. I know you're not on call and I'm sorry to have bothered you, but I need some help here and I don't know who else to call..." *Pause.* "You don't mind that I'm calling? Oh, thank you, sir," and the conversation continued with Dr. Smith describing my symptoms to Dr. Thomas.

Finally, "His wife is coming to take him to the hospital. I will have him meet you at Emergency as quickly as possible. Thank you again!"

And right at that moment Kathie walked into the examining room. "It looks like you're going to be taking me over to El Camino Emergency," I said.

"Okay" she said, "What's going on?"

I explained as quickly as possible what had transpired, and then Dr. Smith came in to tell us that we were to meet Dr. Thomas at El Camino Hospital Emergency as soon as we could get over there. As he left the room he turned around to say, "Dr. Thomas wanted me to tell you that he would have to put a tube down your throat, but not to worry; he is one of the best in the world at doing that procedure."

I smiled, thanked him for his hard work, and we were on our way. During the drive over I mentioned to Kathie that we would probably have a long wait in Emergency before I'd be seeing the doctor. "You know how it is this time of night."

When we arrived, Kathie left me off at the door and I waited while she parked the car. Then we walked into Emergency, and I told the nurse at the desk my name and that I thought we were expected.

"Mr. Fregger!" and then turning her head she hollered, "Mr. Fregger is here!"

All at once there was a gurney with a nurse and two aids holding intravenous setups. They pushed me onto the gurney, shoved the needles into my arms, started the flow of saline solution, and then rolled me down the hall into an examining room. Kathie came along and said, "Well, that didn't take so long."

A few minutes later a doctor came into the room. "I'm Dr. Thomas." he said. "How are you doing?"

"Fine," I said.

"I am going to have to find out what is going on down in your stomach," he said. "But I have decided not to use a tube."

I felt some relief that I wouldn't have to go through that procedure again.

"I've decided to use a television camera instead," and he smiled.

Relief short-lived.

"Don't worry, I am really very good at this," and with that he left the room.

A couple of minutes later two nurses came in, each holding a hypodermic needle. The head nurse said that her needle contained sodium-pentothal, while the other contained a valium solution.

"We're going to put the drugs into the saline solution. In a short time you're not going to care what the doctor does to you," one of the nurses said.

As the drugs entered my system, I felt myself drifting off to never-never land.

When I regained consciousness, I was sitting up in some sort of operating studio with a something down my throat.

"How are you doing?" Dr. Thomas asked.

"Just fantastic," I slurred, filled with the high that was being produced by the combination of the two drugs injected into my bloodstream. "You can stick tubes down my throat anytime you want to," I mumbled.

The next thing I knew, I was back in the examining room. Dr. Thomas was waiting to talk with me. When he saw I was awake, he said, "You have a 'gusher' down there. The ulcer is so bad your blood is being pumped into your stomach. I could actually see it spout each time your heart beat. We're going to have to operate immediately. I've already called a surgeon."

"Wait a minute," I said. "I have no doubt you're right about the bleeding, but if there is going to be surgery, there is only one surgeon that operates on this body. So you can tell the surgeon you've called that he doesn't have to come down."

"Who is your surgeon?" he asked.

"Dr. Joseph Ignatius," I said.

Dr. Thomas paled, "What if he's out of town, and we can't reach him?"

"First, let's see if he's available."

Five minutes later he was back. "Dr. Ignatius' exchange says he is unavailable. It is important we operate tonight. I should arrange for that right now."

"I don't think the emergency is that great. I'll make you a deal. You put me into intensive care and watch my signs. I know there are drugs that slow down bleeding. If you haven't been able to stop the bleeding by tomorrow morning, I'll let you operate. If the bleeding does stop, we'll wait until Monday and try to reach Dr. Ignatius again. If he is still not available, I'll go with your surgeon. Okay?"

He looked at me for a few moments and said, "Okay," and left the room. In a few minutes the nurses returned and I was on my way to intensive care.

⸻

Kathie told me later that when Dr. Thomas came back from trying to call Dr. Ignatius, he came up to her and said, "Your husband is a very sick man; he's lost three quarts of blood, and he won't let me operate. He says he wants Dr. Ignatius and I can't reach him."

Kathie couldn't believe she'd heard him right. (She'd never heard of someone losing three *quarts* of blood.) Her automatic response was to laugh.

"It's not funny. Your husband is bleeding to death."

"I'm sorry, I didn't laugh because I thought it was funny. I've just never heard it said that way before. Brad usually knows what's best, and he has strong opinions. I'd suggest you talk it over with him."

Dr. Thomas looked at her for a moment and finally said, "Okay."

The next morning, the day nurse came running into my room with a look of concern on her face. She stopped when she saw me and said, "I was looking for Mr. Fregger. The chart said he was back in this room."

"I'm Mr. Fregger. But this is my first time in this room. Maybe you mean my father; he's also in this hospital. Was he in this room recently?" I knew my dad had been in intensive care, but I didn't realize I was in the same room (actually the same bed) that he had been in just one day before.

"So Rolly's your father. You gave me a start! He has had such a tough time, and when I left I thought he'd finally made it. Then I saw your name on the chart and thought it was his, and that he was back again."

I thanked her for her concern and asked her what room my dad had been moved to. Then I gave him a call.

"Hi, Dad." I said.

"Hi, Brad. What are you doing?"

"I'm lying here in bed taking it easy."

"It's Saturday, isn't it? Aren't you going to do something special today?"

"Well, actually the bed I'm lying in is right downstairs. I was admitted to the hospital last night and I'm in intensive care right now—the same room you just vacated."

"My God! What happened?"

"I was feeling kind of weak, and it turned out that I have a bleeding ulcer and have lost a lot of blood. It looks like I'm going to have to have my stomach operated on sometime in the next couple of days."

"How are you feeling right now?"

"I'm feeling fine. I don't think there's anything to worry about." We talked for a few more minutes and then we hung up.

I found out later that after hanging up the phone, my dad had burst into uncontrollable sobbing and cried for a long time. He cried for his son and the operation he was going to have soon. During the course of his recovery his doctors had told him that if he thought he had it tough, he should be glad he wasn't having a stomach operation, "Stomach operations make heart operations look like a cake-walk."

Now he just found out his son was in intensive care, waiting to have a stomach operation.

But he also cried for himself, something he hadn't ever been able to do. He had had a very rough time and, in fact, came very close to dying. He had needed the therapy that comes from a good cry. From that moment on he began to get well, began to live again. I honestly believe that, without that cry, his healing process would have taken much longer, and he might never have healed fully. As it was he has healed fully and is still living the life of a healthy, vibrant individual. Part of me believes that this was the reason I had gotten sick at this time; my dad needed help to survive, and this was the only thing that would help.

On the following Monday I got through to Dr. Ignatius, told him what was going on, and he was at my side within the hour. They operated on Tuesday, September 10th (Kathie's and my wedding anniversary) and the operation was a success.

The operation had been a major one; Dr. Ignatius had taken half my stomach and cut the nerves that control the flow of acid into it. Still, I felt ready to be released within the week. I also didn't like what they were feeding me, and I told the doctor I could do better myself. He agreed, so I was released from the hospital one week after the operation. I went home to be in charge of my own recovery.

One week later, I went to Dr. Ignatius to see how I was doing; and after the examination, he proclaimed, "You're completely well! It's been an almost miraculous recovery. You're free to go, free to eat anything you want." Then he started to laugh.

"What's so funny?" I asked.

"I wish I could have seen the look on Dr. Thomas' face when you told him, 'Nobody touches my body but Dr. Ignatius,'" he said. "If everyone would take responsibility for their own health like you do, we'd have a lot less problems."

I thanked him for the compliment. Then as he was leaving the room he turned to me and said, "I *am* the best there is when it comes to stomachs."

"I know," I said, "Why do you think I insisted on having you?"

He looked at me, smiled and left the room.

I got dressed, went home to pick up Kathie, and then we went out together for lunch, a hamburger at Burger King. It was one of the most delicious hamburgers I have ever had, and I had it exactly two weeks after my operation.

Shanghaied

There are many ways you can *seize the moment.* You can seize it even when very bad things happen, when you're sure your life must be over. Instead of feeling sorry for yourself, you can begin to look for a solution, for alternatives, for a way to make the best of it. You can be a Brodie Lockard....

One afternoon in July of 1984, a couple of months before my medical crisis, I got a call from Caratha Coleman, the wife of my boss Ken Coleman.

"Brad, you need to meet Brodie Lockard. He works over at Stanford University. I talked with him and was very impressed. I'd use him myself if I could get him away from Stanford, but there's slim hope of that."

I thanked her and then called Brodie at work immediately. We made arrangements to have breakfast together the next morning.

"We'll have to choose a restaurant that can handle my wheelchair."

"How about Stickney's at Town & Country Center in Palo Alto?"

"I've eaten there. That's perfect."

"8:00 am too early?" I asked.

"I can be there," Brodie said.

"See you tomorrow morning then."

I hung up the phone and promptly forgot about it. I mean I forgot the appointment entirely.

I always kept my appointments. But this time I forgot and wasn't reminded of it until that next afternoon when I got a call from Brodie.

"Brad, did I get the wrong day? I was at Stickney's this morning until nine…you never showed."

There was a long pause as I digested this. *Did I really forget that appointment?* You bet I had. I was very embarrassed. "Brodie, what can I say? I forgot. I don't know why, but I forgot. I'm sorry."

"It was a great inconvenience. It isn't easy for me to get out that early. I don't like to do it for nothing."

He wasn't going to let me off of the hook easily, and I didn't blame him.

"I'm very embarrassed and honestly sorry. Is there something I could do to make up for it?"

Silence on the other end of the line.

"Could I come and see you right now, drop what I'm doing and come right over? Will that work for you?"

Again silence.

Finally, he said, "I guess that would work. How soon can you be here?"

"You're at Stanford University…I can be there in twenty minutes."

"Make it half an hour. I'll meet you in front of the Hoover library. Do you know where that is?"

"Sure do! See you in half an hour."

I hung up the phone and was on my way.

I was there first and had a short wait before Brodie arrived. He was a bright, good-looking young man, about twenty-four years old. He had a large shock of blond hair cut in a casual style that reflected the Stanford surroundings. He had told me that he needed a restaurant with access for his wheelchair. What he didn't say was that he was a quadriplegic.

He had been a Stanford athlete until the fateful day he had broken his neck on the trampoline.

Brodie took his circumstances in stride. In the beginning I had a problem doing the same, especially when I instinctively held out my hand to shake his. It was obvious that this was something he couldn't do.

I liked Brodie from the beginning, and we had a wonderful conversation, talking mostly about learning (educational) software and a few other things. But it didn't look like we were going to be able to work together.

At the end of the conversation, I told him, "If you ever have an idea for a game, please give me a call first. I'd love to take a look at it, maybe even publish it for you."

About six months later, on December 17th, 1984, Brodie called.

"Brad, this is Brodie Lockard. Do you remember me?"

"Of course. What's up?"

"I have a game I want to show you."

I was very busy getting ready for the Consumer Electronics Show in Las Vegas. But my curiosity got the better of me, plus there was the residual embarrassment of the original missed meeting. And, of course, I had promised to take a look at his game, "maybe even publish it." The only free time I had until the middle of January was Christmas Eve morning. That was fine with Brodie.

On Christmas Eve morning I drove over to his house in Redwood City and was warmly received by his mother, Dorothy. She took me into the living room where Brodie was waiting for me. He was in his wheelchair next to a table that had his Macintosh on it. But the Mac wasn't facing Brodie; it was facing the center of the room. On a coffee table in front of Brodie was a stack of tiles. I took the chair that had obviously been set aside for me to sit in.

Brodie asked, "Do you know what these tiles are?"

"Mah Jong tiles," I answered.

Mah Jong tiles are about the same size and shape as dominoes. The best are made of ivory and have very beautiful designs cut into them. They are used to play a four-player game called Mah Jong, which is like a "rummy" card game. This game is very popular in the far east and has also been popular here in America from time to time. The tiles on Brodie's coffee table were stacked in an unusual way.

He explained that it was the opening stack for an ancient solitaire game called *The Turtle* that had been invented in China a few hundred years ago.

The objective of the game was to remove all of the tiles from the stack, leaving an empty board. You had to remove the tiles according to a couple of simple rules. It was great fun, but setting up the stack each time you wanted to play was a real hassle.

Brodie had programmed the game so it could be played on the Macintosh. In this way the computer built the stack each time so the player didn't have to.

The first time I saw it I was greatly impressed. By using the Mac, he'd created beautiful graphics; and *The Turtle* appealed to me immediately. The game was simple but wonderful, a compelling challenge people would probably want to play again and again. I said as much to Brodie.

Now I was going to have to see how good it *really* was. I'd be wasting my time if the game wasn't fun, fun for a lot of people. To do this I needed to take a copy with me, but Brodie didn't like that idea.

"I don't know...(pause)...I don't want to lose control. I've worked on this for a long time. I wouldn't like it if something happened and the code got out."

"It's hard to proceed without taking a good look. I can guarantee that I will take personal responsibility for your program. I will know where every copy is, and I will get every copy back if we're not able to make a deal."

Brodie looked over at his mom. I saw her shrug her shoulders. I imagined the conversation,

What do you think?

I don't know. It's your decision.

I waited while he thought it over.

"You'll take personal responsibility?"

"I guarantee it."

He finally agreed, as long as I would sign a simple non-disclosure.

"Sure. Do you have it handy?"

"It will just take a minute to get it ready. Can you wait?" I nodded. "Mom, can you give me a hand?"

Dorothy came over and moved the computer so it was facing him. Then she picked up a rod of some kind with a mouth-piece on one end, which she put into his mouth. Brodie then bent over the computer and began using this rod, or stick, to press the keys. He brought up his word processor, opened the file he needed, and then began making the additions. Everything was accomplished by using the mouth-stick and pressing one key at a time.

It was at this moment that the immensity of his accomplishment hit me. He had developed *The Turtle* in just this way—pressing one key at a time with a stick he held in his mouth. He had programmed the entire game, created all of the graphics, done it all — one key press at a time. I was amazed.

Later I would see a picture of Brodie taken before his accident. He was in position on the parallel bars, his form perfect, his body healthy. I felt a sadness that he couldn't have always been that way, but I didn't feel pity. Brodie didn't allow pity. He had programmed *The Turtle* as therapy. He had *seized the moment*, he had accepted this unexpected, unwelcome turn of events, accepted the facts of what he could no longer do, and began discovering what he *could* do.

***

The first person I showed *The Turtle* to was my wife, Kathie. She didn't like computer games, so I thought she'd be a good test. If she showed any interest at all, it would be worth further exploration. Kathie saw the program for the first time Wednesday night, December 26th, in our kitchen (I'd set up the Macintosh on our kitchen table). I showed her basically how it worked and then left to watch television and do some reading.

About 11:00 pm I told her I was going to bed. She said she'd be right there. I woke up during the night and noticed Kathie wasn't in bed. I looked at the clock and saw it was 5:00 am.

I hollered out, "Kathie, are you here?"

From the kitchen, "Yes."

"Is everything all right?"

"Yes."

"Are you coming to bed?"

And she gave me, for the first time ever, an answer that would be heard millions of times around the world.

"I'll be there in a minute. I just want to play *one* more game."

I began to think we might have something here.

The next morning I took the program into work and talked to an associate of mine, Sam Nelson. "This is a new program I'm thinking about licensing. Would you mind taking it home for the weekend? Maybe you could find some time to take a look at it."

"No problem, we're not doing anything else."

"This one's real confidential. Don't show it to anyone except Paula. I gave my personal guarantee."

"Gotcha."

On Monday morning, he came into my office and asked, "Can I borrow your Macintosh?"

"What's wrong with yours?"

"Paula wouldn't let me bring it to work. She wanted to play *The Turtle*. We didn't do anything all weekend but play that game!"

Now I knew we had something special.

The contract negotiation turned out to be much tougher than I expected or it should have been. And it was my fault. I tended to side with the developer when it came to contracts, and I wanted Brodie to get everything I thought he deserved for bringing this wonderful program to the world. So I negotiated with the company the best deal we had ever done with an outside developer. And then I went to see Brodie, *sure* he would be impressed by what I had accomplished on his behalf, and *anxious* to sign this wonderful contract.

But Brodie didn't know about my efforts, and he wasn't very happy with the concept of accepting the "first offer." What a mess! I had already pushed the company to the limit, and now our developer was saying it wasn't enough. Ultimately, Ken Coleman got involved and was able to make some considerations that made Brodie happy, but I had learned my lesson and never again did I leave myself in a position from which I couldn't move.

We, Activision, had decided the game was good enough to move to other systems, so my next job was to find the people to do these other versions. The program looked so simple, really was simple. But the programmers I found, time after time, had problems duplicating Brodie's work on other computers. I had to fire the entire first group, when after three months they still didn't have something playable on the screen. This was when I first discovered that scientific and business application programmers often don't have the skills necessary to program entertainment products at the level our customers expect. Most "high level" programmers assume games are easy to do but, it turns out, leading-edge games are an extremely difficult programming challenge, one that only the top ten percent of programmers are up to.

Finally I got most of the programming started, only to have a problem with the marketing people. They tried to write the marketing plan without playing the game. They wanted me to tell them what they needed to know. I put my foot down and refused to talk to anyone who hadn't played *The Turtle* for at least half an hour. I didn't do the bosses any favor; within a short time, we had a whole department addicted to the game.

As you can imagine, I had strong feelings about the game, including feelings about what it should be called. I was in favor of "*Addiction*." I thought since it was essentially an adult game, the name *Addiction* wouldn't hurt it. But the industry had just finished another round of bashing by those people who were afraid we were losing a whole generation to the "addiction of computer games," and the company was concerned with that title. Ultimately marketing came up with the name *Shanghai*, and I learned why they're in marketing and I'm in product development. The name *Shanghai* was perfect. It spoke of being "captured," and it had an oriental flavor just like the game.

To my credit they did say in the advertising materials that *Shanghai* "was addicting" and that phrase did end up giving the product a lot of good free publicity. It worked just like I thought; since the game was seen as essentially an adult product, the term did not end up being threatening. The reviewers said things like, "Activision calls *Shanghai* addicting... I doubted... I was wrong. I haven't gotten any work done for three weeks. You have got to try *Shanghai* from Activision."

Within that first year, *Shanghai* won almost every entertainment award, and became one of the most played computer games in the world, selling over ten million copies in all of it's variations. I was happy, Brodie was happy, and our judgment as to the kind of computer game people of all ages would enjoy was affirmed. And when industry experts talk about the lack of computer games for women to enjoy, they most often start, "With the exception of *Shanghai*..."

This story began fourteen years ago, but *Shanghai* is still selling and selling well around the world. This is unheard of in the computer games business, where you're extremely lucky if your game stays on the shelf one year. This unequalled success is in spite of the many unauthorized versions available. For example, you may know the program as *Tai Pai* from Microsoft. This was the first of three of my programs

Microsoft copied. One of the reasons for the continued success of *Shanghai* is its appeal to men and women of all ages and cultures.

❦

I moved to Austin, Texas, a couple of years ago, and during the first few weeks a friend took me to a local show called Ester's Follies.

After the show we were walking down sixth street, where all the action is, and she suggested we step into the Forbidden Fruit Tattooing and Piercing Salon.

"I bring my college sex education class here on a field trip once in awhile," she said.

My curiosity got the better of me, and I agreed.

The first thing I thought when I entered was, "I have *nothing* in common with these people."

Then I noticed a black man behind the counter at the back of the store with more rings through him than I believed possible. He had rings in his ears, his lips, his nose, even multiple rings in his eye-brows. Again the thought surfaced, "This guy and I have nothing in common." As I walked up to the counter I noticed he was working at the computer. I said, "What are you doing?"

He responded, "Playing *Shanghai*."

❦

All of this happened because a young man *seized the moment*, refused to accept defeat, and had the personal strength to rise above tremendous adversity. Brodie's commitment, courage, and ability to live with the facts of his life have been a continual inspiration to me. I have had the privilege of working with him many times over the years. In addition to *Shanghai*, a couple of years later he programmed

Solitaire Royale on the Macintosh for me, and provided some exceptional graphics for *Ishido*. He has been a good friend and associate. I thank God for the day I met Brodie Lockard.

And now, "the rest of the story." I told you I had problems getting the right people to program *Shanghai* for other computers. Well, the Macintosh version had been out almost three months before the IBM version was done. On the day the "ship decision" was made, I received in the mail, unsolicited, an IBM version programmed by a sophomore at the University of Colorado in Boulder, Michael Sandige. I put the disk into my computer and up came a version of *Shanghai* that, in many ways, was better than the one I had just decided to ship.

The letter said, "I saw the Macintosh version in the software store I work in, and I liked it so much, I took a month and put this IBM version together. My friends thought it was good enough for me to show to you, and that you might be interested in marketing it."

One month! And I had spent the first three months just trying to find someone with the skill needed to move it to the IBM. Well, after our lawyers wrote Michael a letter stating very clearly that his version should not be distributed to anyone in anyway, I decided to stay in touch with this young man who seemed to be so talented as a programmer. That association has been extremely rewarding also, but that's another chapter.

Portal  *Chapter 11*

While *Shanghai* was the high point of my time as a games producer for Activision, there were other products and stories that stand out in my mind.

Early on I got an idea that we ought to try an interactive novel. Written novels are almost always extremely linear in approach. They have a beginning, a middle, and an end, with a lot of stuff (action or drama or comedy) in between.

I wanted to try something different—a novel that could be read in many different ways, from many different paths. In order to do this I needed a writer, but not just any writer. I needed a writer who could think in non-linear fashion.

The first few writers I interviewed couldn't even understand what I was talking about. I began to believe I would never find the right one when somebody suggested Rob Swigert.

Rob taught at San Jose State University, where I left a message for him. The next day we were talking on the phone. I was explaining my basic idea, "...so it needs to be non-linear. After all, we do have a computer here. There's no particular reason why it needs to be read in any specific order. But the writing might be a bit tough."

"Not for me," he said with confidence. "That's how I think. My problem is trying to keep everything linear so I don't confuse my readers too much. You need to read *Little America*. I'll get a copy over to you right away."

"What's *Little America*?" I asked.

"It's a novel I wrote. When you read it, I think you will agree that I can handle a non-linear approach to writing."

We made an appointment for lunch for the next week. I needed to talk to him face-to-face. Everything was sounding pretty good over the phone. What would he be like in person?

At lunch I was convinced I had found my writer. We immediately developed one of those creative relationships that feed off each other in a fantastic sort of way. Anything either of us said would push the other even further. I was sure I had found what I was looking for.

That night I went home and read *Little America*. That sealed it. Now I knew Rob was the perfect writer for my experiment in the interactive novel. *Little America* was the most non-linear book I had ever read. It was a wonder anyone could follow it. This was a masterpiece of a whole new genre of literature. With him writing our interactive novel, it was bound to be a masterpiece in its own right.

Rob quickly put together the basic scenario for our story. An astronaut had been on a long space journey and was finally returning to Earth, expecting to find civilization intact. Instead, he found an empty planet. However, the computer system still worked, and by exploring the system files he was able to determine what went wrong, and ultimately save humanity. The player, of course, was the astronaut.

What made it non-linear was that the files could be explored in any order. This meant it was a slightly different experience for each player. It was truly a masterpiece. We called it *Portal*.

We now had two-thirds of the team necessary to bring *Portal* from concept and story to finished computer game. We had the author, Rob Swigert, and the producer, me. But we didn't have a developer. I had really started backward with this project. Normally all ideas came from programmer designers. Then it was up to the producer to find the resources necessary to bring the project to completion. This time I had the concept and story but no programmers.

I was getting concerned about this when Rob called, "Brad, a friend of mine up at the Institute for the Future wants us to drop by and explain what we're doing to some of the researchers who work up there. What do you think?"

The Institute for the Future is a high-level consulting group that helps companies deal with long-term future issues. It's a highly respected organization. I had become aware of them when I was pursuing my Master's Degree in Futuristics from San Jose State University. I had always wanted to visit them and find out what they were about.

"Sounds terrific. When do you have in mind?"

Rob suggested a time a couple of days from then that worked for me. We met at the Institute, and he introduced me to Paul Saffo, one of their directors.

After a short getting acquainted time Paul said, "What you're doing with *Portal* is very interesting to us. We have used novels in the past to try and share our vision of the future, with surprising effect."

"Tell me more," I said.

"For instance, we were working with a company that wanted to know the potential long-term effects of certain decisions. We determined that these decisions could have significant environmental consequences and mentioned that in our report. The company received the report, but the individuals didn't seem to grasp how important these decisions were." He paused for a second. Then his eyes looked up, visualizing what he was about to tell me.

"We decided to do something dramatic, so we contracted with a writer to write a novel based on the situation, a novel that would graphically describe the potential impact on the environment of what they were about to do. Then we sent the novel to the management committee's wives," he paused and looked directly at me before continuing.

"Can you guess what happened?" he asked.

"I would think you got your point across," I answered.

"Better than we ever believed we would. The wives insisted the decision be changed. The executives didn't have a choice, not with that level of lobbying. It turned out to be an extremely effective technique, one we have hesitated to use again."

"Why?" I asked.

"It was just too powerful," he answered.

We talked for awhile about future studies, the Institute for the Future, and then he took us around for individual meetings with other senior consultants. When we were done, Paul met with us one more time.

"Thanks for coming. Be sure to keep me up-to-date on the progress of *Portal*," he said.

"We will. Thanks for having us," I responded.

"By the way...do you have a developer yet? Whose going to program it for you?" he asked.

"I haven't found one yet, haven't really started looking. Why do you ask?'

"There's a young group of programmers getting started in San Francisco that I'm familiar with. The founder is a bright guy just out of school. I think they would be perfect for you. They seem to be very creative, very willing, and very hungry. Would you like to meet them?"

"Sure. If they work out it will be the final piece to the puzzle. The team will be in place, and we can begin development. When can we do it? The sooner the better." I was anxious to get started, to move on to the next step and begin planning what *Portal* would look like on the computer.

It turned out we were able to get together the next day.

I was surprised to see that this new company was in a neighborhood in San Francisco. In fact, we drove up to a beautiful three story San Francisco home. The young founder had taken over his parents house to start this new software development company.

It was unbelievable what the parents had done to help him

get started; they had literally given up their home. All of their furniture, in every room (except for the master bedroom) was pushed up against the wall and covered with sheets to keep the dust off. Temporary tables and desks had been brought in, and young college aged kids were sitting in front of computer screens, working on programs of one kind or another. There were programmers at work in the living room, the dining room, and most of the bedrooms. I was never sure what they were working on. I don't think they had a contract yet. We met in the kitchen at the small table...no computers there.

⚜

This reminds me of a story told to me by my good friend, Raymond Pole, a few years later. Raymond was an expert on power supplies, and one day he got a call from a young entrepreneur who needed a power supply for a new product. Raymond went to see him, and the only place they could meet was at the kitchen table. Raymond told him everything he knew about power supplies, their cost, best place to purchase, etc. When he left, Raymond wished Steve Jobs good luck with his new product, the Apple Computer.

⚜

The four of us sat around the kitchen table and Paul introduced us to Gilman Louie, the founder and president of Nexus. Then, Rob and I described what we were trying to do with Portal, how we envisioned it as the first in a new genre of computer entertainment software, and how important it was for the player/reader to be able to experience the product in many ways, down many different paths.

Gilman caught on immediately, and very quickly the twosome that had been Rob and I became a threesome. The ideas began to flow. The vision that Rob and I had of a novel that would be experienced on the computer in a very special new way started to take shape as Gilman's passion for the concept joined ours, and he began to describe what it would look like on the computer screen.

I now knew the team was in place, and the computer novel *Portal* would be completed. It would only be a matter of time before it would take it's place in the history of computer entertainment.

Portal received more press than any program Activision had ever produced up to that time. The stack of press clippings stood almost four feet high. It was touted as a brand new development, the first of a whole new genre in computer entertainment. It was compared to *2001*, and didn't come out wanting.

After we finished the program, Rob was contacted by his publisher who wanted to publish the book version of the software program. As far as I know, this was the first time that a software game had been the inspiration for a published book. *Portal* was the first of a kind in more ways than one.

It wasn't long after this that we (all of us at Activision Product Development) were back in Chicago at the Consumer Electronics Show (CES). I was flying high, believing I was the most successful games producer in the world. I had some justification for this belief, since the majority of Activision's sales at the time were coming from products I had produced. In a little over two years, I had produced fifteen original titles, fifty-four separate products. I knew of no one else in any company that had done as much.

The only thing missing...I wasn't Vice President of Entertainment Software. Activision didn't have one. We had a VP of Application Software, and a VP of Sports Software, but we didn't have a VP of Entertainment Software. I had hoped I might be chosen, might be promoted to this new responsibility.

We weren't at CES for very long, when Ken called me to his hotel room for a private meeting.

"Brad, we're thinking about promoting you to VP of Entertainment Software, but we've got a couple of concerns." He paused, didn't say anything for a moment or two. Then he continued, "We're not sure you would make a good VP. You don't seem to have the same kind of drive Scott has. He'd do anything to make sports software successful. It would help if you were more like him."

Now I didn't know what to say. Here I was producing more successful software than the other three producers and two VP's combined, and Ken was saying I should be more like Scott, show the "same kind of drive Scott has."

"I don't know what you're talking about. I'm me, Scott is Scott. If I'm not what you want for the VP of Entertainment Software, then don't promote me. But don't ask me to become a different person. I can't do that." I wasn't happy, and I could feel my voice beginning to rise. I shut up.

"Well, I just wanted you to know. Let's forget it for now. We can discuss it again when we get back."

I left the room, went directly to my own room and called Kathie. I needed to share this with someone. It was during my conversation with Kathie that I realized the ride was over, that my perfect job had come to an end. It was either be promoted or stagnate. I couldn't become more like Scott, and I didn't have the personality to stagnate. It didn't look like there was an acceptable alternative.

Then without warning I was sobbing out loud. I couldn't control myself. I cried and cried, with Kathie trying her best to console me. But I wasn't consolable. I had glimpsed the end of the dream and my heart was broken.

Immediately after the phone call with Kathie, I had to attend a Product Development managers' meeting. I know from the glances I got they suspected I had been crying, but thankfully, no one mentioned anything.

When we got back from CES, Ken offered me the VP of Entertainment Software position. I told him I would think it over and let him know.

When I saw him the next day, I said, "Ken, I don't think you want me to be VP of Entertainment Software. It's really not my thing. I'm a maverick. I seldom support management. I wouldn't be happy. I think I'd like to turn the promotion down."

Ken was surprised, "Okay, but I think you might be making a mistake."

A couple of days later, he called me into his office.

"Brad, we think you're right. We think a VP position wouldn't be right for you. Here's what we want to do. We want to create the new position of Senior Producer. You'll be at the VP compensation level, with all VP perks. In addition, you'll have carte blanche. You can develop anything you like, experiment in any way you desire. And you'll report directly to me. What do you say?"

It sounded great...a raise, a prestigious position within the organization, and the opportunity to produce anything I wanted. Who could ask for anything more?

"I'll take it, and Ken, thanks for believing in me."

He smiled at me, we shook hands, and I left his office, excited about this new turn of events. Carte blanche sounded good. It seemed there was an acceptable alternative after all.

Part Three
ON OUR
OWN

Getting Started   Chapter 12

I thought being made Senior Producer with the authority to make any game I wanted would satisfy me. It seemed like a dream come true. I loved so much creating exciting, compelling product that stretched the power of the computer, as well as the imagination and the potential of the player. But down deep something was missing.

I remember so well the day Kathie and I were having dinner with our close friends, Dick and Diana Aldrich. I was sharing with everyone my feelings about the new job, "I don't know, I feel kind of empty inside."

"When did you start feeling this way?" Diana asked.

"As soon as I discovered my future at Activision was limited," I said with a touch of sadness. "When Ken suggested that to be promoted to Vice President I'd have to become more like Scott, the wind just went out of my sails. I lost all enthusiasm."

"What's wrong with Scott?" Dick asked.

"Nothing's wrong with Scott. He's a terrific Vice President of Sports Software." I paused for a second, trying to put words to what I was feeling. Then, "It's just that I operate differently, and maybe the way I operate works great when you're producing product, but breaks down at the Vice President level. I don't know, but that's why I turned down the Vice President of Entertainment Software position."

We all sat silently for a minute. Then I continued, "I should be happy now that I'm the Senior Producer, and I can make anything I want to. But I'm not."

Then Diana said, "If you could do whatever you wanted, what would you do?

It didn't take me long to answer that question, "I'd start my own business, offering producing services to companies in need of product, and being a publisher of last resort for those wonderful products that can't find a publisher to take them to market."

Dick and Diana looked at each other and then Diana said, "We'd like to help you get started."

"What do you mean?" This conversation had taken a turn that I didn't expect. I wasn't sure I understood what she was saying.

Then Dick chimed in, "Let's form a corporation to produce and publish computer software, with the four of us as equal owners. You do the product development, marketing and sales, and I'll handle the finances."

"And I'll be the office manager," Diana said. "I'll provide support so you can concentrate on making beautiful product."

I looked at Kathie, who hadn't said much through all of this. "What do you think?"

"You haven't been happy these past few weeks. I think you'd like being in charge of your own thing. I think you can make it work. Let's give it a try!" she said, her voice full of confidence.

Can we really do this? Wow! For one of the few times in my life, I was speechless.

I'd always dreamed of having my own business. I remember once being told, "When you're facing death, you never regret the things you did, but you often regret the things you didn't do." I knew when I heard that, that I'd regret never having had my own business.

This need is probably in my genes. My grandfather never

worked for anyone but himself, at least since he had come to the United States. And my dad and mom also had a business of their own, a drug/souvenir store in Virginia City, Nevada. I played with the idea momentarily just before coming to Activision. Now it looked like this potential regret was going to be eliminated, and I could die happy, knowing I had at least given it a try.

And during the follow-up conversations, where we put numbers to our plans and reality to our dreams, I realized that while I didn't want to be a Vice President for Activision or anyone for that matter, I did want to be President/CEO of my own company. I had a deep down confidence I could make it work, justify the faith Kathie and Dick and Diana had in me.

Within a week I told Ken about our plans.

"Are you sure you want to do this?" he asked me.

"Absolutely!" I said.

"Okay. We're going to miss you, but I understand your need to have your own business. If you ever need my help, don't hesitate to give me a call," Ken said.

"Thanks for everything. This has been a great ride!"

It was only one or two days after I left Activision when my old boss Tom Lopez came into town for a conference. We decided to meet one night for drinks and conversation.

"So you've taken the leap," Tom was saying.

"I have, and I would be lying if I told you I wasn't worried."

"What are your plans?" he asked.

I started by telling him my plans for *Byte Size*, how I thought it was critical to develop applications that were both simple and effective. "It's crazy how hard it is to use something as simple as a word processor," I explained. "There isn't any reason for it. There are all kinds of neat things you can do with a computer, if only there was software available to do it, software the average person could learn quickly and use easily. We've got to do this if we expect computers to be accessible to everyone, if we expect everyone to get excited about computers!"

I could feel my passion rising. "I can already see a gap developing between people who know computers and people who don't. If this continues we will have a new class society in America, maybe even the world, with the computer savvy people on the top and the rest of the world serving them. This is completely unacceptable and unnecessary. Computers and computer applications don't have to be difficult to use, but in the main they are. I'd like to help change that." I sat back and took a deep breath.

"It's going to take you awhile to accomplish all of that," he said. "What are you going to do in the meantime, to make some money?"

This brought me back to the real world.

I gave a little laugh to cover my embarrassment at being caught philosophizing when he had asked a serious question about how I was going to start my business. And then I said, "I'm serious about getting *Byte Size* started as soon as possible. But while I'm developing those applications, I'll be looking for publishers who need product. I'll also try and sell a concept to a publisher and then develop the product for them."

"Do you have any ideas?"

"Two," I responded. He motioned for me to continue, "Remember *Music Studio*?" He nodded, "I've been talking with Ed Bogas, and he is sure we can make an outstanding consumer music program that will make it possible for most people to create their own music. I'm excited about this. I remember how much fun *Music Studio* was, and I'd love to do something even better."

I took a deep breath and continued, "I have this idea for an exploration product for children." I could feel my passion rising once more. "The product is built around a large, probably haunted, house. What the kids do is just explore the house, no ultimate goal, just pure exploration. There are lots of surprises, puzzles and small games, but they have to be discovered. I think it would be wonderful."

"What makes you think kids would like it?" Tom asked.

"I've been talking with some teachers who use software as a reward when students do well. They have a number of games that take place in computer worlds. These games have goals, but interestingly enough, the teachers tell me most of the kids ignore the stated goals and spend their time exploring, trying to see what they can find. It makes sense to develop a product designed for that kind of activity. I'm convinced this kind of product would stimulate curiosity and imagination. I can't think of two more important characteristics for going forward confidently into the future."

"Sounds interesting. I have one last question, and then I have to go."

"Shoot," I said.

"How much money do you have set aside?"

This was an embarrassing question. Most experts say you should have at least a year's salary set aside before you consider starting your own business. I hadn't taken their advice.

"A couple of weeks' salary," I said sheepishly.

"Good!" This was not the response I expected.

I gave him a questioning look and he continued, "When I left Activision I had a year's salary in the bank. It took me a full year to make my first sale. "Then he grinned and added, "Somehow, I don't think it's going to take you that long."

⟨⟨⟨ ⟩⟩⟩

Starting our own business was the most challenging and most difficult thing we ever did. All of a sudden I was master of my own fate. This was great, but it also meant I couldn't blame anyone else when something went wrong. Before, I was always quick to let the boss know when a bad decision had been made, and then describe graphically the results of that decision. Now I was the boss; there was nobody else to blame when things went wrong.

Another thing I noticed for the first time was the relationship between the money that came in and my efforts. When I had worked for other people, I had never really seen that relationship. The work I did was one thing, the money I received, usually automatically deposited in my checking account twice a month, was another. Now it became obvious; no effort, even unwise effort, on my part, and no money. It seemed like I couldn't afford to slow down, not even for a minute.

I had been worried about whether or not I would have the initiative to get to work on time, whether I would have the discipline I thought was necessary to succeed. It turned out the only thing I had to worry about was taking time away from my work. I could work from early morning to late at night and never feel tired.

It also helped that Diana joined me right from the start. She set up a desk in our family room and was there all day, answering phones, filing, making sure I had the things I needed to do my job.

Dick was taking care of all of the finances, but he didn't quit his job as purchasing manager for Intel. He was responsible for all purchases of over $50,000, and he'd been with them for years. In fact, he had been with Andy Grove and the rest when they were still at Fairchild; it was difficult for him to even think about quitting.

The first order of business was to come up with a name. Since we had two major goals, our first thought was to have two different names, one for our development business and one for our publishing business. We ended up with Software Resources International for development, and Publishing International for publishing. Publishing International became the parent company, with Software Resources International acting as a division.

We had a company and we had a name. Now all we needed was some business, and that was all up to me. I knew what I wanted to do. I began contacting publishers, talking with executives I knew, about what I was doing and how I thought

I could help them.

Tom Lopez was right. I made my first sale in two weeks! The Learning Company was looking for someone to do the Macintosh version of *Reader Rabbit*, a very popular and successful children's program. I convinced them I could handle it.

The next day I was at their offices in Menlo Park, collecting our first official milestone payment as a company. It was an exciting moment. When I opened the envelope, it contained the check to begin *Reader Rabbit* and a note from John Powers of The Learning Company along with a dollar bill. The note said, "Here's a dollar bill to frame. Congratulations!" I greatly appreciated this thought.

I contacted Gordon Walton, who I had gotten to know when I was with Activision. He had a small software development company and did excellent Macintosh programming. After discussing the project, Gordon and I agreed on how we were going to get it done. Basically he and his team of people would do the project, while I was responsible for producing it. I did all of the communication with The Learning Company, and I made sure the program was up to the standards needed to be critically successful.

There was only one slight glitch. Gordon had chosen a fifteen year-old boy, Dale Homburg, to do the artwork for the project; and while he was extremely talented, he didn't have quite the skill I was looking for. Luckily Joan, the computer artist, was available to give him some lessons. We flew the kid to San Jose, and he spent a couple of days with her. By the time she was through teaching him her "tricks," Dale was more than capable of doing what was needed.

The Macintosh version of *Reader Rabbit* shipped on time and on budget. But, even more important, it was an excellent version Macintosh customers loved.

Haunted Houses   *Chapter 13*

The Learning Company told me they were interested in seeing any proposals we might have that would interest them. It just so happened I had a project ready to show them, *The Marvelous Mansion*.

This did not turn out to be an easy sell. They are an extremely goal-oriented company and had a very difficult time conceptualizing a product without a specific goal. I was continually asked questions like, "What, beyond exploration, is the child trying to accomplish?" Or, "What skills or lessons are we trying to convey here?"

I was finally forced to do a relatively major research project with a number of teachers in the San Jose area. It was designed to show the value of pure exploration in the intellectual growth of the child. I think it might have worked for a Master's thesis. The important thing it did was convince The Learning Company to fund the design specification.

I chose to work with Joan and Mark Mathis, to do the design for *The Marvelous Mansion*. It took about a month, but when we were finished, we had the finest design specification I had ever seen. It did everything I had imagined.

It provided a computer world that was

both fun and exciting, a mansion that had been left vacant and was just a little scary. Inside the mansion were all kinds of surprises, games, puzzles, fun and exciting activities; but the child had to find them, had to search and explore to discover them.

Finally we were ready to turn over the final design to The Learning Company. It seemed to me we had a hit on our hands. I was very excited about taking the next step, convinced they would be contracting with us to do the actual development.

One week went by, then two, then three, and we still hadn't heard from them. I was beginning to get nervous when we finally got a call from their in-house producer.

"Brad, I've got bad news. We've decided not to go ahead," she said.

"Why not?" I asked.

"We already have a castle game, and we think that having two games in the market that use abodes would confuse the customer."

"But your castle game isn't anything like *The Marvelous Mansion*," I said with some frustration.

"That's true, but we can't take a chance that the customer will understand. I'm sorry, but that's the way it is."

So my first design went up on the shelf, and our first product development was still in the future.

I haven't given up on *The Marvelous Mansion*. To date I have shown it to three other publishers; but, so far, I haven't gotten enough interest to begin development.

Truth be known, I'm not a good salesman. I don't have the thick skin needed to succeed in that profession. When somebody says "No" to me, I say "Okay" and go away. If someone says, "I'm not interested," I say, "Who needs you anyway!" and walk away. This type of attitude doesn't work if you're a salesman.

I have redone the design three times. The first time was when a publisher told me he was, "...looking for a great haunted house design." I thought I could turn *The Marvelous Mansion* into a haunted house without too much trouble. So I got together with Michael Feinberg, a producer/designer I knew from Activision, who had formed a design company called Magic Partners with a friend of ours, Bobby Levin; and we wrote the design specification for *The Haunted House*.

Again, this was a fantastic design, the perfect design for a haunted house game based on all the fears and excitement surrounding haunted houses. We were able to license this product to Spectrum Holobyte; even had it under development, when it got caught in a corporate decision to quit doing games and focus instead on flight simulators for the military.

I didn't give up. When we had another opportunity, I changed it again and *The Haunted House* became *Beatlejuice...* and then it became *Casper the Friendly Ghost*. This has continued right up to the present; just last year, GT Interactive, one of the largest games publishers in the world, took a serious look at *The Haunted House*. But still no sale.

This is the one regret I still have; I have never been able to produce either *The Marvelous Mansion* or *The Haunted House*. These are two wonderful programs, ones I know people all over the world would love and enjoy, but they are yet to be realized.

Tetris

Chapter 14

About this time I met with Doug Carlston at Broderbund. I was trying to feel him out for the kinds of products he was looking for. We never got far in these discussions. In the main, Broderbund looked for finished product. In their guts, they didn't like the development process all that much.

Most of their major products, i.e. *Paint Shop* and *Carmen Sandiego*, were brought to them almost finished. They could then edit them and send them out to the world. They liked the book publisher model.

During this particular conversation, Doug said, "I've got a simple product here I'd like you to look at and evaluate for me. Our programming staff love it, play it for hours...I don't know."

He gave me a copy and I took it home to play with. It was fantastic. It was simple to understand, fun to play, extremely challenging, and you lost yourself in it, would play it for hours without even realizing it. These are the characteristics of a classic computer game.

I called him and told him to license it right away. "Don't let this one get away from you. If you do, you'll never forgive yourself."

"Thanks, Brad, I'll think about it."

Later on, I mentioned to Gilman Louie at Nexus that I had seen a wonderful product I thought would end up being a classic. He asked me about it and seemed somewhat interested. He was considering merging with a small Denver, Colorado, publisher that was looking to join forces with a strong developer, and they needed a product to get them off to the right start. This was the beginning of Spectrum Holobyte.

The next time I saw Doug was at the SPA (Software Publishers' Association) meeting in Berkeley. The agent for the new game was attending the meeting as well.

"Did you license *Tetris* yet?" I asked him.

"No, do you think I should?" he asked.

"What have I been saying? Of course, you should! But you better do it quick. Robert is here, and he's selling hard.

"Okay, let's do it!" And we started looking for Robert.

Then I saw Gilman coming toward us.

"Hi, Doug. Brad, you know what I just did?" Gilman said. I shook my head, still looking for Robert.

"I licensed *Tetris!*" Both Doug and I looked at him in disbelief.

Tetris has become one of the great classic computer games of all time, famous the world over. You win some and you lose some, and Broderbund won a lot of them.

I'm a little embarrassed to tell the rest of this story. After Gilman licensed *Tetris,* he came to me and asked me to do a design for the commercial product. I told him I would and worked up a design that took advantage of the way the game looked when it was finished; I called it *Mosaic Madness.*

I then presented this design at a design meeting at Nexus's offices in downtown San Francisco. The session went well, and I was proud of my design. About a week later, I was visiting them and Gilman asked me, "You want to have lunch?"

"Sure. Where do you want to go?" I asked.

"Great place a couple of blocks up. We can walk it."

During our walk Gilman seemed to be struggling with something. Finally I said, "What's on your mind?"

"*Tetris*," he said.

"What about *Tetris?*" I asked.

"I don't want to use your design." He stopped walking, faced me directly, and then continued, "I think it would be better to capitalize on the fact that it was developed in Russia. I want to use a Russian theme."

"Gilman, it's your product. Do what you want."

"I know. I just didn't want to hurt your feelings. I wouldn't have a company if it wasn't for you."

"You're not hurting my feelings. Thanks for the compliment, but you're one of the best product development people I know. Now we'll see how good you are at marketing."

The rest is history. What a fantastic start for what was essentially a new publishing company. But every time I see Gilman, he points his finger at me and says, "*Mosaic Madness.*"

Solitaire *Chapter 15*

It was the 1986 holiday season. From just before Thanksgiving until just after my dad's birthday in February, my folks came and visited us from Montana. We spent a lot of time together, most of it playing cards. How my dad loves to play cards!

"Where's Martha?" my dad was saying. "Are we going to play cards tonight or not?" ·

"She's out in the family room playing *Shanghai*. She told me she was only going to play one more game."

"All she ever does is play that game. You'll never catch me spending hours on the computer playing some stupid game."

What a challenge, I thought. *Can I come up with a computer game that my dad won't be able to stop playing?* As we all sat down at the table, I couldn't stop thinking about what it would be...then it hit me...he loves to play cards...how about a card game? Computer solitaire? That's it!

The more I thought about it, the more sense it made. People love to play solitaire!

How convenient it would be if it was on the computer, ready to go whenever they wanted to play. An added advantage would be they wouldn't have to deal or shuffle, the computer would do that for them. And, as we had learned from *Shanghai*, they could play during a coffee break. They didn't have to set aside an hour or two, like you did for most games.

The next day I called Gilman Louie, who was now the Chairman of Spectrum Holobyte; he was responsible for product development. The founder of Spectrum Holobyte, Phil Adam, was President and responsible for sales and marketing. This was a perfect marriage. Gilman was one of the best when it came to product development, and Phil was the best sales and marketing guy I knew in the computer entertainment industry.

Phil had taken a little submarine simulation called *Gato* and convinced retailers across the nation to buy and promote it. He did this without any lucky publicity or connections. I am re-impressed every time I think about it. Then when Gilman licensed *Tetris*, Phil handled that marketing and sales effort as well.

"Gilman, I've got a great idea for a product. When can I come in and talk to you about it?" I asked.

"I've got some free time on Wednesday. How's that?"

On Wednesday I was in Gilman's office waxing poetic about the potential of card solitaire on the computer. "...and people won't have to shuffle. I know they'd love it."

"I'm not so sure," Gilman said. "Shuffling and laying out the cards is part of what solitaire is, at the worst it's a small inconvenience. I'm not sure they'd pay money to play it on the computer," he responded.

"But we learned from *Shanghai* that people love games they can play at a moment's notice and play for just a short time if they want. Plus they loved that the tiles were shuffled for them." I said.

"You can't relate building the turtle to shuffling a deck of cards. I don't know...I'll tell you what, you convince Phil. He's the guy whose going to have to sell it. If it's okay with him, I'll go along."

Phil was available. Gilman left us with a parting comment, "Brad's got an idea for a game; I'm not sure about it. I told him it would be okay with me, as long as you supported it."

"What's this idea, Brad?"

I went through the whole explanation again, but each time I did it, I got better. "...we could offer a lot of different solitaire games, different decks of cards and different backgrounds. People love beautiful things on their computer screen. We can make it look real pretty. What do you think?"

"Actually, I think I'd like it personally, but that's a dangerous assumption on which to invest in a new game. The question is can I sell it, will people pay money for it? You're asking me to invest in something I'm not sure of, even if I do think I'd like it myself."

"What if I accept some of the risk? I'll do it basically for royalties. I will need a new computer for my PC programmer; his current one isn't up to the task. But that's all I need. And I'll do the Macintosh for the same price, but I don't need a computer. Does that help?"

"Sure makes a difference. All we have to pay up front is a new computer for your PC programmer? You're sure of that?" he asked.

"I'm sure. But you've got to do your best on the sales and marketing front. That's the only reason I'm willing to do this. I've heard about what you did for *Gato* and I know what you did for *Tetris*. I want some of that action. Deal?"

"You've got yourself a deal." He held out his hand and we shook on it.

Doing a speculation deal for a computer software product is not a good idea. But, and this is the rationale people always use when they accept this kind of a deal, I knew it would work, knew we would win in the long run.

What a team! Working with Brodie again would be a delight—he'd program the Macintosh version. Then there was my brother, Dennis, a commercial art major who'd worked with Joan (the computer artist) on the original ClickArt. I knew the art would be beautiful. I'm still playing this game today, programmed over eleven years ago.

Mike Sandige, of course, was that young college student from the University of Colorado who whipped up a version of *Shanghai* in a month. He would program the PC version.

Yep, this was one terrific team.

There are hundreds of different solitaire card games and people play by many different rules, but there was never any doubt as to which games I was going to include. And when it came to rules, as far as I was concerned, the ones I learned as a child were the only rules to play by.

When I was growing up, I'd often visit my Aunt Anne. One of mother's six sisters, Aunt Anne was a very special person, and while I couldn't except everything she believed or did, I loved her dearly. Aunt Anne started every day by playing what she called, "my game." She would play eight solitaire games (Pyramid, Golf, Klondike, Canfield, Corners, Calculation, Three Shuffles & a Draw, and Reno) in a row and keep a running score. When my brother and I visited, we'd play against her for best total score. Aunt Anne almost always won…she cheated…I still loved her. This would be the design for the first computer card solitaire game.

I wish I had some story about how difficult the development of the first card solitaire game was to complete, how we coalesced into a team and defeated the enemy, bringing out the product just in time for the holiday season. But it didn't happen that way. The development went very smoothly, and *Solitaire Royale*, published by Spectrum Holobyte and developed by Publishing International, was shipped on time for the holiday season, 1987.

With the introduction of *Solitaire Royale*, we succeeded in destroying the spare time (and not so spare time) of millions and millions of people around the world. Recently, Microsoft told me their research has shown that card solitaire is the most played game in the world. I don't doubt it. Over the years people have told me time and time again, when they discover my involvement with card solitaire, that hardly a day goes by they don't play...which brings me to another story.

A few years later, I had a design meeting at my home for a product we had licensed to Disney. It was called *Heaven and Earth*. Present at the design meeting were Michael Feinberg, lead designer, who I knew from Activision (and who played a significant role in other Publishing International products), Scott Kim, puzzle designer (one of the top puzzle designers in the world and the inventor of a style of writing called "Inversions" that is literally mind-blowing), Ian Gilman, Macintosh programmer (one of the top young Macintosh programmers around, so good that Apple asked him to consult with one of their R&D groups on the proper use of the Macintosh interface), Mike Sandige, PC programmer, and Mark Ferrari, artist (without a doubt one of the top games artists in the world), and myself.

It was about 11:00 am, and I noticed that Mike Sandige kept checking his watch.

"Are you in a hurry to go someplace, Mike?" I asked.

He looked uncomfortable, afraid that he was interrupting the design meeting. Then he said, "Well, I'd hoped we might take an early lunch. There's something I'd like to do during lunch."

"What's more important than what we're doing right now?" Michael Feinberg asked in an impatient voice.

"Orson Scott Card's going to be at the Sunnyvale Town Center signing his latest book. I wanted to get one."

"Why didn't you say so!" three of us said in unison. "Let's go." And before you could say *Ender's Game*, we were all on our way out the door to meet Orson Scott Card. We were determined to *seize the moment*. The design would wait— Orson Scott Card wouldn't

When we got there, the line extended to the back of the store and around to the other side again. Orson Scott Card was a popular author with the Silicon Valley set. We hadn't been in line too long before Scott Kim said, "While I'm here waiting, I might as well do an Inversion for him.

We thought that was a great idea. Besides we loved watching Scott write them. An Inversion is a style of writing where the word, phrase, or most often, name is the same whether viewed upside-down, or right-side-up. It isn't a mirror image; it's the same name whether seen right-side-up or upside-down. I know it sounds impossible, but he could do it.

When we got to the head of the line, I was first. After Orson Scott Card signed my book, I waited around for Scott to give him the "Orson Scott Card" Inversion.

"I did this for you." Scott said.

Orson Scott Card took it, saw his name on a piece of paper in a weird writing style, and then looked up at Scott with a questioning look on his face.

Scott reached out, took hold of the paper and turned it around. He said, "You're looking at it upside-down."

Orson Scott Card did a double take, and then exclaimed, "Oh, you do these, too?"

I said, "What do you mean, 'you do these, too?' He is these!"

"I've seen things like this in *Scientific American*," he explained.

"Meet the man who did them," I said. "Scott Kim meet Orson Scott Card, Orson Scott Card meet Scott Kim."

"Wow, this is great!" Orson Scott Card said.

Then Mike Sandige, the next in line, said, in an "I'm better than you are" tone of voice, "You didn't get to see him write your name like I got to see him write mine."

Orson Scott Card looked over at him and then back at Scott, "Do you mean you just write these, you just sit down and write them?" He didn't sound like he believed that was possible.

"Yes, that's what I do," Scott replied.

"Could you write one for me right now?"

This is what Scott had been hoping for. He loved the pressure of having to do an Inversion on the spot with everyone watching. "Sure, what do you want me to write?"

"How about two of them, one for each of my children?"

"My pleasure. What are their names?"

The line still stretched to the back of the store, but no one was complaining. The ones close enough to see what was going on were fascinated. When Scott finished, the line burst into applause. Orson Scott Card beamed as he looked at the names of his children, turning the pages around again and again.

Then he put them away carefully, signed Scott's book with a great salutation, and turned to Mike Sandige and said, "And what do you do?" There was an undercurrent of "can you top that?"

I said, "Well, he programmed *Solitaire Royale*."

Orson Scott Card looked at him with disbelief, "You really programmed *Solitaire Royale?*" Mike nodded and Orson Scott Card continued, "That's my favorite game. I play it every day! I can't tell you how much I love it."

━ ⌬⌬⌬ ━

Solitaire Royale was a boon to our new company. In addition to being the first product we developed that was licensed to a major computer games publisher, it ended up being our introduction to the Japanese marketplace.

While I was still at Activision, we had licensed the worldwide computer game rights to the movie *Labyrinth* from George Lucas, and then sublicensed the Asian rights to a major publishing company in Japan, Tokuma Shoten. The way the contracts were written, everyone had creative control; Activison, Lucas, and Tokuma.

Ken Coleman told me, "We've got a little problem we think you can help us with.. All you have to do is get Lucas and Tokuma to agree on a design for the Japanese version of *Labyrinth*."

"Don't forget that I've got five days to accomplish this.

I'm dealing with the egos at Lucas, and Tokuma probably believes they know what's best for the Japanese market, which they probably do. In addition, I don't speak Japanese," I responded.

"That's about it, but we should be able to find a person to translate for you." He said all of this with a big grin on his face. I think he enjoyed giving me these challenges.

The upshot is I did get a great translator, Tom Randolph, who understood the computer games business and the Japanese. Tom was born and raised in Japan, he had an American father and a Japanese mother. He was very good, and with his help we accomplished our goal.

At the time the *Labyrinth* deal was happening, Tom was a student at San Francisco State. But a couple of years later he had his own business and was representing Fujitsu Limited software development efforts in the United States.

Fujitsu is the second largest computer manufacturer in the world, behind IBM. They had developed the finest multimedia computer in the world—perfect for games—and they were looking for software developers to make products for it. And, unbelievably, as far as games developers in the United States were concerned, they were willing to pay.

Tom brought the people from Fujitsu around, and that was the beginning of a very rewarding relationship. These were among the finest people in the world to do business with. Never in all the years I worked with them did they ever break a promise made to me.

Fujitsu licensed *Solitaire Royale* from us, with Mike Sandige doing the programming here in the United States. It was the first game, programmed in the United States, released for Fujitsu's new computer, the FM Towns, and it went on to receive rave reviews from Japanese game magazines.

My only disappointment came when we got our copies of the final shipping product. The FM Towns computer was the first computer in the world that shipped a CDROM with every unit. This meant that all FM Towns products were distributed on CDROM. *Solitaire Royale* took up less than five percent of the available space. Fujitsu couldn't see wasting all that extra memory, so they shipped two products on the same CDROM, This meant the CDROM box had two fronts, one displaying *Solitaire Royale*, and another displaying the other game. I vowed that this would never happen again.

Oh, yes, when the 1987 holiday season rolled around, my mom and dad brought their Mac along with them. At home they fought about whose turn it was to play *Solitaire Royale*. But when they came to our house, Mom could play on my computer, while Dad used theirs…mission accomplished!

Byte Size *Chapter 16*

From the beginning we were determined to create simple, effective applications that would enable more people to get real value out of owning a computer. Our approach was two-fold: first, develop easy-to-use, single purpose applications; second, our major products would be limited in features. Basically, we would only include what was needed by eighty percent of the customers.

By focusing this new line of software on single-need or limited-feature applications, we were able to shorten the development cycle and create effective programs that were easy to learn and use.

We named our new line of software *Byte Size*. I loved this name and everything that it conveyed. In many ways the complete story of *Byte Size* is a book all by itself, a terrific case study for the Harvard Business School MBA Program.

We don't have time for that now. But I will serve you up a few "bite sized" samples to give you an sense of what took place; how a great idea that starts out terrifically can end up such a disappointment. When this happens, you're never really sure why; but you do spend a lot of time analyzing your process, your decisions, and what you might do differently if you had the chance.

The two programmers who helped us build the *Byte Size* line of products, (without them we probably couldn't have done it) were John Blu and John Keene. John Blu had a wonderful little program for tracking stocks. I'd never seen anything like it, and as we were to find out, neither had anyone else.

John Keene also had a terrific little program, but this one was designed to make using MS–DOS much easier. This type of program was called a DOS shell. DOS shells were the precursor to Windows. They displayed the directories and files in an organized way that made certain tasks, i.e. opening programs, copying and/or moving files, or finding lost files much easier. This one was especially neat because it allowed the user to create long file names; this was brand new stuff at the time. Other DOS shells tended to be expensive as well as complicated; ours would retail for around thirty dollars.

Neither John had been able to find a publisher for his program, and they were both excited to finally find someone who wanted to work with them.

These programs were just what we were looking for, simple and effective with all the needed features and very little extras. And they were both using extremely effective menu–driven user interfaces. The importance of this feature was very clear to me. In order to be simple, a program had to be menu–driven.

The success of the Macintosh and Windows is proof of the necessity of this type of interface. Before Windows existed, PC programmers had to write these interfaces for themselves. This was not an easy task and was the reason so many applications at the time worked without menus, or with elementary menus that were hardly any better.

Now we had to figure out what to call these programs. We tried to think of a catchy name, but finally decided that the name *Byte Size* really said it all. There would be no confusion as to what our products did. Our first two products were titled *Byte Size Stock Portfolio* and *Byte Size DOS Shell*.

Since I was so impressed with the work of these two gentlemen, I asked if they could use that same technology to develop some additional applications. They both agreed to give it a try; and in this way, we were able to add *Home Inventory, Recipe Finder, Video Tape Log, Coupon Finder, Modem Software* and *Word Processor* to the *Byte Size* line very quickly. These programs fit our philosophy of publishing a variety of single purpose programs that would fill customers' specific needs.

Within one year of starting business, we had the first thirteen *Byte Size* programs ready to take to market. The packaging, while simple, was elegant and reflected the *Byte Size* philosophy. It had been designed and created by Michael Mathis, who also helped us with *The Marvelous Mansion*.

All that was left was to find a fulfillment house. These are the people who duplicate the disks, put the final product inside the packaging, and then send it off to the customer. The customer is usually a retailer, or software distribution company.

We got our first "employee" when we hired a high school friend of Kathie's and mine, Tom Sunday, to help with all of the things we had to do to begin publishing our own product. Tom and his wife, Dorothy, who was also a high school friend, had been looking to relocate back to the San Jose area. This gave them the opportunity at just the time when we needed someone to help.

It was Tom who discovered Greg Walberg. Greg owned what would be our fulfillment house for the entire time that we were in business. Even more important, Greg believed in us and supported that belief by investing in the company, ultimately becoming an equal partner with Dick, Diana, Kathie and I. A lot of what we were able to do over the years was only possible because of Greg's continued support.

Now we had everything in place, and only needed sales to

bring the dream to completion. We didn't have to wait long. Our first significant sale was to Electronics Boutique, a national software chain started on the East Coast. I had contacted them and arranged to have our product evaluated. We passed with flying colors, and they ordered the entire line for the majority of their stores.

The next sale happened at the SPA meeting in Boston. It turned out to be an easy one. I walked up to Gary Kusin, the Founder and President of another major software retailer, Babbages, and showed him our product. He looked it over; listened to my pitch about easy to learn, easy to use; liked the idea, and ordered twelve dozen of each...all in about three and a half minutes. I called Diana, and the product was shipped to Babbages even before I got back from the SPA meeting.

After the SPA meeting I did a sales trip through the East, meeting with as many retailers and distributors as I could. The response was way beyond expectation, and I was able to write a number of orders for merchandise. It was exciting to see our concept had the immediate support of the distribution channel.

Then we waited to see what would happen. The first chain to actually get product on the shelves was Babbages. Within a week after the product arrived in their stores, we received our first reorder. The immediate best seller was *Byte Size Home Inventory*, with *Byte Size Stock Portfolio* close behind. These two titles continued to be the best selling *Byte Size* products for the next five years.

Very quickly we were in every major software chain in the United States. We were on our way, and the future looked very good indeed.

❦

The response to *Byte Size* was affirming. The concept and the software were well received not only by the distribution channel, but also by the people who purchased it, took it home and put it to use, and by reviewers in most computer magazines.

Reviewers were excited about the selection available, about the opportunity people now had to put their computers to work in some specific ways that made sense. They also were impressed by the fact there seemed to be almost no time needed to learn it, and once you knew how to work one *Byte Size* program, you pretty much knew how to work them all. This meant, in most instances, the user began using the software for its stated purpose almost immediately. For reviewers of PC software, this was unheard of—a first in the industry.

But it was the comments from users we enjoyed the most. Hundreds of people told us their computer had been an extreme disappointment until they discovered *Byte Size*. We received long letters thanking us for making it possible for them to finally write a letter,

"I couldn't figure out how to work any of the word processors that were suggested to me...then I saw the Byte Size Word Processor on the shelf; the price was reasonable...I decided to give it a try. This is my first letter! I wanted to send it to you and thank you for making this possible..."

When you do a mass mailing to customers, you consider it a terrific success if your response is from two to four percent. The only exception to this is when a software publisher does an upgrade mailing for an important application. When we did a mass mailing to our customers, the response ran well over ten percent. Users trusted and loved *Byte Size* software.

We were happy with the progress of *Byte Size*; while sales weren't going through the roof, they were steadily increasing. Then a few things happened that did not work out well for us.

First, Nintendo became the rage and kids were playing video games again. Since video games were sold in toy stores and not computer software stores, customer traffic dropped off in the stores where our product was being sold. Our major customer had been the mom or dad who was in the store looking for a present for junior, a new computer game. They would purchase a *Byte Size* product on impulse and be hooked. Now that customer was going to the toy store to buy their gifts. Our sales suffered significantly.

Additionally, we had started out as path finders, the only publisher offering simple, effective programs to personal computer users. Coincidentally, another publisher with the same basic concept opened shop around the same time we did, not ten miles from us; *My Software* and *Byte Size* both began business in Santa Clara County, better known as the Silicon Valley. But initially *My Software* had a tough time getting into the computer stores.

Then the real competition opened for business, *Softkey*. They also offered a number of single focus, simple programs at great prices. In fact, when they were beginning, they licensed both *Stock Portfolio* and *Home Inventory* from us and then put their own name on it. We didn't mind; it meant royalties for us and more people having software that they could use. *Softkey* would eventually become one of the largest software publisher's in the world; they know how to do business.

Competition is always a problem, but in this instance it became a very big one. The major problem was their packaging was much better looking than ours. By now ours was five years old, while there's was fresh and new. Because of the design, ours tended to be stocked with the spine out, making it difficult for the potential buyer to see it. Their's was almost always stocked face forward, so the potential buyer had no trouble finding it. This was a problem we had to solve.

The only solution was to redesign our packaging, bring it up-to-date. Sounds simple but we estimated the basic costs of doing the design and manufacturing of the packaging at $100,000. We didn't have that kind of money. If we had ever had a smash hit, a million unit seller, it wouldn't have been a problem, but we never did. We had broken new ground, and then we had sown the seeds. Now it was time to harvest, and we couldn't afford a tractor. We needed one; our horse had died!

We flirted with the idea of getting some venture capital. A good friend introduced us to one of the top firms in the Silicon Valley. Dick and I arrived at their offices on a Wednesday afternoon.

If you've never been in the offices of a venture capital firm, you can't imagine the feeling of wealth and success that permeates it. The conference room we were shown to looked like it had been built for a movie about the rich and famous. The carpet was a light gray and very plush. The table was of rich mahogany, dark and freshly oiled. The chairs were soft and comfortable, but designed so you could easily work at the table. We were impressed.

We set up our equipment, prepared for our demonstration, and waited for Timothy Applet, the senior partner with whom we were going to meet, to join us.

Finally he entered the room. He was young, no more than thirty-two, well-groomed, and had an attitude about him that radiated professionalism. He got right to the point, "What have you got to show me? Harry said you were worth talking to."

Harry had been my contact to this firm.

"It was nice of Harry to recommend that you meet with us," I said. "Let me show you what we have that I think has the chance of changing the way computers are used, of convincing the vast majority of non-computer users that it's now time for them to buy a machine."

With that I launched into a presentation of our *Byte Size* line of product.

Timothy interrupted the presentation after only about five minutes.

"What's this BS about simple and easy to use?" he said.

I was confused. This was the first time anyone had suggested this might be a bad idea.

"Computers and software are relatively hard to use. This is

why most people haven't taken the leap yet," I responded.

"That isn't true. For crying out loud, even my two year old daughter can use my Macintosh. What *are* you talking about?"

He seemed frustrated, that he was wasting his time with someone who didn't know how easy computers were to use since the introduction of the Macintosh.

But we weren't talking about the Macintosh; we were talking about MS–DOS machines, i.e. the IBM personal computer. However, it so happened that Kathie and her best friend, Beth Pole, were currently enrolled in a beginning Macintosh class and were having a difficult time figuring out how it all worked. In fact, they both found *Byte Size* software easier to use than the Macintosh.

"I'm talking about PC software, not the Macintosh. However, not everyone finds the Macintosh easy to use and in my opinion, there is a great need for this software on the Macintosh as well," I said.

"You don't know what you're talking about. I was a Macintosh evangelist before starting this firm, and I can tell you that the Macintosh will take over the world. As I said, even a two year old can work a Macintosh," he said very impatiently.

He had pushed my button. All of a sudden I didn't care that we had gone to see him to raise some money. I knew I could never work with this guy. He was blind to what was going on, would never see the value of *Byte Size*.

"I understand what's going on here," I said. "Your mistaken preconceived opinions are making it impossible for you to see the value of simple, effective computer applications. It's you who doesn't know what he's talking about."

He looked shocked, like he didn't believe anyone, especially someone looking for money, would talk to him that way. Then he said, "This meeting is over."

"It sure is!" I responded.

We packed up and left. That was the last time I ever asked a venture capitalist for money.

We were undercapitalized; without the needed money, we couldn't update the *Byte Size* packaging.

This was a problem we couldn't solve, and sales suffered. *Byte Size* didn't die a quick death. It stayed around for almost ten years. We sold over a quarter million *Byte Size* programs. *Stock Portfolio* ended up having the longest life. CompUSA continued to carry it years after all other *Byte Size* products were long gone. They told us they couldn't find a replacement, a program that did what it did so well and so easily.

Publisher of Last Resort

At a certain point in my career as a computer games producer, I became convinced that much wonderful product was not making it onto the retailers' shelves. This feeling was affirmed by my introduction to John Blu and John Keene and to the wonderful programs they had developed that they couldn't get published.

I have seen the same thing happen in other "called" professions. These are professions where individuals must do the work that is their purpose for living.

Often these people are writers, artists, or musicians. Called professions tend to be creative endeavors that usually result in a creative product, a novel, painting or song. It is unbelievable how many talented people there are. It is a shame so much of what they do is seen by so few.

I am especially aware of this in Austin, Texas. Austin must have more creative people per capita than any other place I have ever been, maybe in the world. I have never heard so many fine musicians as I can hear here in Austin on any night of the week. Austin calls itself the "live music capital of the world." I believe it. Here in Austin many make their living playing music; many more must keep their day job. Much beautiful music, music others all over the world would enjoy, is played for the few that have been lucky enough to discover the musician, to find the small club where he or she plays or sings.

I know the same is true for writers. I know because of the stories we hear about the books that were so difficult to get published, the books passed over by publisher after publisher. *Chicken Soup for the Soul*, the Dr. Suess books, *Jonathan Living Seagull*, *Embraced by the Light* are a few more visible examples. Books that, because of the persistence of the author or friends of the author, were finally published and could then be read by millions. How many more wonderful books found their way to bottom drawers when the author couldn't stand the thought of one more rejection letter? What a waste of the creative endeavor, what a loss to the world.

I, too, feel called, called to find a way for some people having trouble getting published to share their creations with the world. When I was dreaming about my own business, I would dream of strategies to offer to the public beautiful software programs that couldn't find a publisher. To find cost-effective, innovative ways to present new, exciting programs to the consumer, programs they would never know about otherwise, to be a publisher of last resort.

Buckminster Fuller tells us that one of the significant advantages of the affluent society is that people have a greater chance to live out their dreams, to be about their purposes. By allowing this, enough of us will do something so significant, so critical to the ongoing success of the society, that it will more than pay for the rest of us to do things that are not as important. I agree with him, but will go even further. I believe that a significant number of individuals, left to their own devices, will add significantly to the lives of others in that society.

Some will create music others will enjoy, even find moving. Some will create art others will want to gaze upon, find peace in contemplating. Some will write, and others in the reading will find affirmation or challenge, a reason to go on living, a purpose of their own. Some will create or invent new things, and these things will make life easier, or make possible things not possible before, or bring to millions, things only a few could share before.

In a small way I was able to accomplish this through *Byte Size*, and through the marketing and distribution of two wonderful little programs whose stories follow.

⟡

I was first introduced to *Crazy Rabbit* in 1983, while I was still with Activision. Ivan Manley sent it around to all of the publishers, hoping to find someone who would publish it. *Crazy Rabbit* was a fun little arcade game with a farmer trying to catch a rabbit who was stealing all of his carrots. You were the rabbit. If you got all the carrots before the farmer got you, you won that level and the right to go on to the next one. There were fifty levels in all. We liked playing it, but we were too involved in our own products to consider publishing it.

Now I had my own company, and it was my turn to try and convince publishers that they should do business with me. I had been out visiting all of the publishers I could find, trying to get a feeling for the kinds of computer entertainment programs they were looking for, when I met Dave Grady, a producer at Electronics Arts. Dave had been assigned to a new project, so the timing was right to bring him a proposal.

Timing is everything. One day you approach a publisher and the last thing they want to do is talk to you about a new game proposal. Then you stop back a week later, and they want to know about anything and everything you've got available. That's why you don't give up, you keep going back. You've got to catch them at the right time.

When you met with people at Electronics Arts, you didn't meet in their office. Most of the time they didn't have one; they had a cubicle in the middle of a bunch of other cubicles. It was a rare person who rated a window. What they did have was a multitude of tiny conference rooms with a table and three or four chairs.

I was sitting in one of these conference rooms one afternoon and Dave was saying, "We're going to start a budget line of game software called Amazin' Software. This was Trip's original name for Electronic Arts."

Trip Hawkins was the founder of Electronic Arts, a legend in the industry. With this name on the line, he'd take some personal interest.

Dave continued, "I don't mean old stuff revisited. What I mean is brand new games offered at a budget price."

"That sounds interesting. Anything special you're looking for right now?" I responded.

"Something in arcade action would be great. But this is going to be a budget line. We can't afford the same level of advances we have for our regular stuff. You understand, don't you?" he asked.

"I don't know if I do or not. It takes the same amount of time to develop a budget product as it does to develop one to sell at regular price, as well as the same amount of testing. What am I missing here?" I asked.

It seemed to me they were trying to get me to cut my prices to a point where I wouldn't be making any money, where it wouldn't be worth the effort.

"I understand that. The best thing would be if you already have a game, one that's fun to play and exciting, but you haven't been able to find a publisher for it. Do you have anything like that?"

Initially I thought, "Nope, this isn't going to work for me." And then *Crazy Rabbit* jumped into my mind.

"I just may have a game for you. It's arcade action and lots of fun, but the programmer hasn't been able to find a publisher. I'll give him a call and see if he's interested."

"Great. Have I seen it?" he asked.

"I don't know. It's called *Crazy Rabbit* and the developer is Ivan Manley. He lives up in the Seattle area."

"I think I remember *Crazy Rabbit*. Didn't it make the rounds a couple of years ago?"

"That's when I saw it." I was beginning to get worried that

he'd go to Ivan directly and leave me out. I didn't want that to happen. This was a great opportunity to begin doing business with Electronic Arts. They were the biggest computer games company in the United States. It wasn't just *Crazy Rabbit* that was at stake—it was the potential future deals we would get if this one worked out.

"You give Ivan a call. If he's interested, I'd like to consider it seriously. We will work through you. I would never have remembered if you hadn't brought it to my attention," he said.

As soon as I got home, I gave Ivan a call. "Ivan, it's Brad Fregger. Do you remember me from Activision?

"Sure. I heard you left to start your own business," he said.

"I did. That's part of the reason I'm calling..." and I told him the possibility we had to license *Crazy Rabbit* to Electronic Arts.

"It's fine with me," Ivan said. "I wouldn't have known about their new venture if you hadn't called. As far as I was concerned EA had turned *Crazy Rabbit* down. Go for it! I'm with you all the way."

So we did a deal with EA for *Crazy Rabbit*. This was to be one of the first games in their new Amazin' Software line and the first original title. We were excited to be given that kind of exposure.

However, there was one small problem; they didn't think a game about a farmer chasing a crazy rabbit around would appeal to the target audience. Additionally, the rabbit used ladders to move between different areas on the farm, and it didn't make sense to them that a rabbit would use ladders.

They suggested we change the rabbit to an explorer, an Indiana Jones kind of character; the farm to a tomb, and the farmer to a mummy or tomb guard. Both Ivan and I liked the idea, so we went ahead with it. Then we changed the name to *Pharaoh's Revenge*. This solved the problem of the ladders; explorers could use ladders. We ended up using both the mummy and the tomb guard. The mummy walked slower and was easier to beat, while the tomb guard was fast, a real challenge.

Pharaoh's Revenge was one fun game to play. There were over one hundred levels, plus a construction set that let the player create levels of their own. I knew we had a great game, as one of the first in EA's new budget line of computer entertainment products.

We had finished the game and they were ready to begin package design. Then three months after the introduction of the first two products, they cancelled the Amazin' Software line without notice, without giving *Pharaoh's Revenge* a chance.

I was getting frustrated. This was my second original product contract cancelled before shipping. First, the *Marvelous Mansion*, cancelled after the initial design was completed, and now *Pharaoh's Revenge*, cancelled after the game was completely finished but before it shipped. One thing I had learned, there were no guarantees. A publisher could cancel whenever they wanted, for any reason they wanted; the developer had no recourse.

At least we had a fully completed product to take around to other publishers. Maybe we could find someone else to publish it.

I tried but I couldn't find anyone interested. What broke my heart was that it was so much fun to play. It was the kind of game people really enjoyed. I felt the players should judge its worth, not a publisher evaluation committee. Mistakes had been made before; hadn't they told George Lucas the public was tired of science fiction movies when he'd brought them *Star Wars?*

I talked it over with Dick, and we decided to publish it ourselves. After all, didn't we think of ourselves as publisher of last resort? Here was a chance to put our money where our mouth was.

This was not an insignificant commitment. What with packaging (design and manufacturing), duplication, marketing materials, etc. our initial investment in the product was over $25,000. While that seems small compared to today's costs, or even to major publishers' expenditures at that time, it was a big thing for us, a major decision.

I wanted to give it every chance to succeed, so the first thing I did was send it off to a select group of computer games reviewers. Since we had some time before we would be ready to ship, and a completed product (a rare thing in the computer games business), I wanted to take advantage of the situation and see if I could get some quotes for the back of the package. This was never done with a new product, there just wasn't time. Reviewers refused to review a product that wasn't finished, and publishers refused to hold up package design and shipping until they could get their first reviews.

I had every hope reviewers would see the value we saw, would like *Pharaoh's Revenge* as much as we did. We were not disappointed. The comments that came back were way beyond my expectation. Here is a sample of the reviews. Oh yes, these were the best reviewers in the industry at that time, every one of them highly respected by peers and publishers alike.

"You won't be sleeping the sleep of the ancients once you've loaded *Pharaoh's Revenge*. In fact, you might find it hard to get any sleep at all...one of the most irresistible and replayable Apple arcade games to appear in ages." —Bob Lindstrom, *A+* Magazine.

"For PC players, *Pharaoh's Revenge* delivers absolute arcade excitement of the *Boulder Dash/Mario Brothers* variety.... This will keep you up all night." —Keith Ferrell, *Compute! PC* Magazine.

"*Pharaoh's Revenge* is the perfect antidote for an overdose of complex, cerebral computer games. It's easy to learn, difficult to master, loads of fun to play—and definitely habit forming." —Celeste Dolan, *Computer Entertainer*.

"I'd forgotten how much fun an arcade game can be. *Pharaoh's Revenge* looks easy, but gets impossible fast. There's something compelling about a game that 'I know I can win, if I play just once more...' —Paul Statt, *inCider* Magazine.

But it doesn't seem to matter what the experts say, even when it's on the back of the box. As a small publisher with one game and a line of budget applications (*Byte Size*), we just didn't have the marketing power of the big guys. We sold about 3,000 units to begin with, but the initial sales to consumers was so slow that reorders just didn't materialize.

It was frustrating to go into computer hardware and software stores and listen to conversations between first time computer buyers and salespeople.

"What do you recommend in games? I'd like to try something that's fun and exciting," the customer would ask.

Invariably the salesperson would answer, "Flight simulators are very popular or, if you want something different, a lot of people really like to play *Zork*."

The customer had specifically asked for something fun and exciting, and the salesperson had recommended a flight simulator (not a game and definitely not fun or exciting—in addition, they are very difficult to learn and not easy to use) and a text adventure, *Zork* (it is a game, but, for most of us, not fun, not exciting, and also very difficult to play).

This was extremely damaging to the computer games industry. These people believed these products were good examples of computer games. The result was they never bought another one, no matter what the reviewers said. They assumed they were being made for an elite group of players that didn't include them.

It was this knowledge that gave me the idea for our last promotion of *Pharaoh's Revenge*, our last chance to make it successful. With the reorders not coming in, I needed a special offer to grab people's attention, something that wouldn't cost any money (we didn't have any left in our *Pharaoh's Revenge* budget).

Then it came to me. There must be thousands of people out there who have been sold flight simulators and text adventures who absolutely hated them, but who believed they were examples of computer entertainment. What I would do was offer a free copy of *Pharaoh's Revenge* to anyone who would send me a letter describing their experiences with flight simulators and text adventures. The idea: "You think you hate computer games, but you've never seen a fun one. Once you see how much fun computer games can be to play, you'll hate them no longer. Try *Pharaoh's Revenge* Free, pay only $5.00 for shipping and handling." The shipping and handling charge covered our basic expenses, and the offer could result in some favorable public relations.

I sent out a press release and got articles in some of the major computer games magazines. Now we just needed to wait and see if there was any interest. We got over 5,000 letters, some of them three and four pages long, from people venting about their frustration with the computer games they had been sold. They were looking for something fun and exciting to play. They didn't mind if it was challenging, in fact expected it, just as long as it was fun.

We had really pushed a button. There were plenty of people out there who had been led astray. The good news—we were able to send them a fun game to play. We made a lot of people happy, but it wasn't enough to save *Pharaoh's Revenge*. I had learned a new lesson. This sales and marketing stuff was damn difficult, especially if you were a brand new, relatively small company with very few products.

⚓

I first saw *Hometown, U.S.A.* at a Consumer Electronics Show (CES) in Las Vegas. Sam Nelson took me out on a balcony. He didn't want anyone else in the room to see what he was about to show me.

He said, "I want you to see this new product Ivan and Carol have. I think we should license it, and I want your opinion."

It was a terrific creativity program that let the user build 3D model buildings. Perhaps you're familiar with the heavy paper books you can buy that have a building in them you can cut out and then quickly and easily assemble into a model. Ivan and Carol's program put a variety of these buildings on the computer so the user could print them out and then build the buildings. But, and this was the great part, it also had the tools and templates needed so the user could create buildings of their own design.

Sam had licensed it and was well into development when Activision decided it was too great a risk, too hard to market. Marketing and selling a new concept product is probably one of the most difficult things in the world to do. The consumer doesn't have the time to stop and figure out what a new product will do for them. It's got to scream its purpose in a short, simple sentence a person can understand immediately.

This isn't true just for computer software. It's hard to sell anything new. That's why the big companies tend to redo what's successful over and over again. It's a better bet in the long run. Of course, we don't get much new that way, but you make a big mistake to ignore this fact of life. If you're determined to bring something new to the world, you should at least know what you're setting out to do is going to be difficult. And you probably won't succeed.

The term for simple to understand ideas is "high concept." The best explanation I've heard is this. You're a movie producer running from one sound stage to another at a big movie studio. You've got a great idea for a movie, and you see a fellow producer running toward you (he's also late for a meeting). When he gets close enough, you holler, "Got a great new movie idea."

"What's it about?" he quickly says.

Then as you pass, without slowing down, you describe the movie to him in less than ten words.

"Sounds terrific, include me in," he shouts as he continues on his way.

That's high concept.

This neat new program from Ivan and Carol was wonderful, but it was not high concept. It would be very hard to describe to the consumer.

❦

It was shortly after *Pharaoh's Revenge* was finished that I got a call from Ivan Manley asking if I would be interested in trying to find a publisher for *Hometown, U.S.A.*

Hometown, U.S.A. was created by both Ivan and Carol Manley. Ivan did all of the programming, including a graphics program that let the user easily create buildings of their own. This was important for the PC version of the program because, at that time, graphics programs (paint and/or draw programs) were not in common usage on the PC. For the Macintosh version there was no problem. The Macintosh came with a paint program called *MacPaint*, and that was all the user needed to print out the hometown buildings we shipped with the product, or create building after building of their own design.

It was Carol who did the design of the all the buildings included, as well as the templates for walls, and roofs, and windows, etc. that made it easy for the user to go off in their own direction. Carol's graphics were wonderful, and the results exciting and, for most people who didn't think of themselves as being very creative, surprising.

It turned out the best possibility we had for licensing *Hometown, U.S.A.* was with Disney Interactive Software. I made three trips to Southern California trying to finalize the deal with them. The plan was to rename it *Disneyland, U.S.A.* and recreate all of the buildings so that children and adults could create a Disneyland of their own, right in their home.

On one of the trips, Disney gave me free run of Disneyland to take pictures of all of the important buildings, from all angles, so Carol could recreate them for the program. The one we chose as a demo, to show the power and capability of the program, was the Disneyland Train Station. Carol did a terrific job; when you built it, your station looked just like the one in pictures from Disneyland.

I was optimistic we would license it to Disney. It was perfect for their product line. It was a creativity program (a natural for Disney), it advertised one of their most important products (Disneyland), and they needed some excellent product for their line.

Again, it wasn't to be. I never really discovered the final reason they didn't do the product, only that, "It isn't quite right for what we have in mind." During some early conversations, I heard some concern from Disney's legal staff about allowing users to have plans for the Disneyland buildings. I thought I had overcome that concern by telling them we weren't using building plans. There was nothing anyone could get from our buildings that they couldn't get from a picture. But, I'm sure that concern played a role in their decision.

Here we were again; a terrific product and no one to publish it. I talked to Dick. He was concerned about the cost. Then Kathie and Diana got involved and said, "We have to do this. It's much too wonderful to let die." We bit the bullet for the second time. Again, we played the role of "publisher of last resort."

I'm not sorry we made this decision. We did get *Hometown, U.S.A.* into stores both in the United States and Japan. Thousands of people discovered the product and were overjoyed at the results they were able to attain.

One man wrote to say it provided him with a way of announcing the birth of his new son that had never been done before. Included with the letter was a model of a movie theater he had created—on the outside a billboard with the birth announcement, and inside on the screen, a picture of his new son.

A school district in California gave the program to their fourth grade classes where the students studied the missions. The kids used it to recreate some of the missions, and in the process learned more about the California missions than any of the classes in years previously.

The schools that discovered the program loved it. A class of mentally challenged students used the program to create buildings for a large map of the area, as a way of teaching the students how to get around town. It was very successful.

I was most surprised by the letters from architectural firms that said that they were using it to create initial models to show prospective clients. Previously the creation of these models had taken hours and was very tedious. Using *Hometown, U.S.A.*, they saved most of that time and found they were having fun making the models.

The most excited people were the ones whose hobby was model railroads. *Hometown, U.S.A.* was made for them. It allowed them to create models for any size railroad, easier than they had ever been able to do before. But if your hobby was model railroads in 1990, you probably didn't have a computer, not yet anyway. Without a computer, our program was worthless. However, we still made a number of model railroaders who did have computers very happy.

Even with all of this interest, sales were barely keeping ahead of expenses. If we didn't have a breakthrough pretty soon, we wouldn't be able to continue selling it. The big problem was you couldn't tell from the packaging that you could use the program to easily create your own buildings, even a model of your own home. We had tried our best, but we had failed to bring that critical point across.

This time I thought I knew what went wrong, why *Hometown, U.S.A.* didn't sell as well as I believed it would. What we needed was some way of showing a model already built; maybe a package modeled after those pop-up cards with a front flap that opened. When the customer opened the front flap, a model building would pop up, graphically illustrating what the product could do. Then the customer would get the idea.

Actually, I used the concept of showing a completed building when we asked the members of the Software Publishers' Association to vote for *Hometown, U.S.A.* as the Best Creativity Program, Educational Category, for the year 1988. I had nominated the program (publishers or developers had to nominate their own programs) and we had been chosen as one of the seven finalists. If you're a finalist, it is expected that you will provide a free copy of the program to all of the SPA members. It was also expected that you would ask for their vote at the time you sent them the program.

When we sent the program to them, I included a simple model building. They received the box, took out the building, and then took out the product, *Hometown, U.S.A.* With the building in hand, there was no confusion. I talked to associates from the SPA years later who still had our model building on their desk or in their bookcase.

I'll never forget that luncheon at the SPA meeting in San Diego, California. I had almost not attended lunch, but a meeting I had scheduled was cancelled. As we were sitting there, the SPA president came to the microphone and announced that they would be giving away some of the SPA Excellence in Software Awards at lunch, "We don't have time to give them all away at the awards banquet tonight."

Then I noticed a listing of the awards to be given away on my table. The Best Creativity Program, Educational Category was included. It all seems a fog now. I could hardly believe it when he announced, "And the winner is... *Hometown, U.S.A.* published by Publishing International."

I don't remember how I got to the podium to accept the award, or the short speech I gave, hopefully thanking those that had made it possible, including Carol and Ivan Manley. The only thing I do remember is standing there looking out at the audience, in shock with the realization that *Hometown, U.S.A.* had won the highest award given in the software industry, akin to winning the Academy Award or a Grammy. What a fitting ending for a wonderful program. It was an award well deserved.

The Way of Stones   Chapter 18Chapter 18

These next two chapters are devoted to a little known but wonderful game many people have found as compelling as *Shanghai*. This game is a story of *seizing the moment* in almost every possible way. We are dealing here with the development of a computer game, but much of what is chronicled will be familiar to anyone trying to "make it" in today's business environment.

I first met Michael Feinberg when he came out to Activision to interview for a job. He was just finishing his MBA from Ohio State University. I liked him right from the start, so he was hired as an associate producer working under my direction. Michael is an extremely talented individual who seems to interact with the universe in a special way that most of us don't understand.

About a year later, Activision had another layoff and Michael found himself without a job. He wanted to stay in the computer game industry so he teamed up with some friends of his who were working with Timothy Leary to design a computer game based on a theme coined by Herman Hesse, "*The Glass Bead Game*." Every person in the group had an ego as big as the state of Texas.

About a month into the project, February of 1988, I got a call from Michael.

"Brad, can I come right over? I've something I want you to see."

"Sure, I'll be here all morning."

When Michael arrived he looked like death warmed over. "You look terrible...what's the matter?" I asked sincerely.

"I haven't had any sleep in the last three days...I'm exhausted, but I couldn't wait to show you what I've been doing," he said.

This was one of the times I had my office in my home, so we went into the living room and Michael began to take some pieces of cardboard and a simple game board out of his briefcase.

"Remember I told you I was working with Timothy Leary on *The Glass Bead Game*?" I nodded and he continued, "Three nights ago I dreamed the game, and when I woke up the entire design was in my mind. I've spent the rest of the time getting it down on paper and then finally building a prototype. That's what this is," and he pointed at the stuff he was spreading out on my coffee table.

Then he took a slim document out and said, "Here's the design. It explains the game concept. It's a very simple game...I call it *Stones*," and he handed me the document.

He was right, it was simple. It took me about five minutes to read the entire design. The game itself was extremely interesting. It didn't seem like a new game...no, much more like an ancient game, like a game that had been around for centuries, like *Chess* or *Go*.

"I like it," I said. "Can I get a sense of it from the prototype?"

"Oh yes, the prototype plays just like the game will play on the computer. Here, give it a try," and he pushed the game board in front of me.

Stones was the same kind of game *Shanghai* was. I call these types of games "meditative strategy." They are extremely strategic in nature, but have no arcade or "adrenaline producing" quality. *Shanghai* and computer solitaire are the two most famous examples. This is the one computer game genre that is equally loved by men and women, as well as the young and the old.

Both *Shanghai* and *Stones* use *Mah Jong* type tiles and a game board. The major difference between the games is with *Shanghai*, you start with all the tiles on the board and, following simple rules, try to take them all away; while with *Stones*, you start with an empty game board and, following simple rules, try to put all the tiles onto the board. With *Stones*, you score higher when you place the tiles in very elegant patterns.

I played for awhile, then looked at Michael, shook my head, and said, "This is the finest game I have ever seen. It's a masterpiece! I have no trouble believing that people will still be playing it a thousand years from now."

Michael sighed deeply, sat back on the couch, and I watched all of the tension drain out of him.

"You don't know what it means to hear you say that," he said. "I had no way of judging how good it was...it just came to me...I wrote it down as it came to me."

"Someone has given you something wonderful. It sure feels like *The Glass Bead Game*...use beads instead of tiles." We sat there silently for a minute or two, just thinking about this wonderful jewel that Michael had been handed by the gods. What a gift!

Michael went off, confident he had the game in hand that would become known throughout the world...*The Glass Bead Game*.

About a week later I got another call from him.

"I just tore up the design and trashed the prototype." He said with no introduction, not even a hello.

"What are you talking about?" I asked.

"*Stones...The Glass Bead Game*...whatever," he replied.

"What do you mean you tore up the design, trashed the prototype? What would make you do that?

"They hated it. They said it was awful, that it would never work. They told me the best thing I could do was destroy it," he said angrily.

"Then they're stupid," I said. "Actually, I'm not surprised.

With that group of egos, I'd be surprised if they ever agreed on a design for the game. But why throw it away? It's still a great game. For crying out loud, if you're going to throw it away, throw it my way. I'll take it."

"You want it? You got it. I'll be right over."

And, sure enough, thirty minutes later he was knocking at my door.

"Here it is. It's all yours."

He handed me the design and the prototype, and then immediately turned around and walked off.

At the time, I had no idea where all this would lead...thank God.

I put *Stones* on the "back burner" after Michael gave it to me. I was already extremely busy with the projects I had going. There was no time right now for a new one. Then about six months later, Michael called to say he had gone to work for Gilman Louie at Spectrum Holobyte as a producer, and that it looked like we had a good chance of doing *Stones* with them.

"Are you interested?" he asked me.

"Sure. What do I need to do?" I asked.

"Nothing right now. I just wanted to be sure that it was okay with you if I pursued it."

"No problem...after all, it's your game," I said.

"No it's not. I gave it to you."

"Whatever," and that was that for the time being.

This meant that *Stones* was the fourth game of ours that Spectrum Holobyte was considering. They were already publishing *Solitaire Royale*, and we had one other game under development, *Haunted House*. They were also seriously considering an interactive mystery novel on the order of *Portal*.

It looked like we were fast becoming a development arm

for Spectrum Holobyte. This was a great opportunity; it looked like we could stop beating the bushes and concentrate on doing what we did best, develop product.

Wrong again. This was when Spectrum's parent company demanded they leave games behind. Within a short time, they quit publishing *Solitaire Royale*, canceled development on *Haunted House*, and chose not to consider either the interactive mystery or *Stones*. Oh yes, and Michael, as a producer of computer games, was once again out of a job, but not for long. The next thing I knew he was at a computer games company called Epyx, and *they* wanted to do *Stones*. With Michael doing the selling, we were bound to do it sooner or later.

Michael had been working on the design, and had decided to call the product *Ishido*. This is a made up Japanese word, which is a difficult thing to do. Japanese is basically a frozen language, which means the concept of creating new Japanese words is pretty much unknown. This is one of the reasons they embrace other languages so easily and also why their language is peppered with modern English terms. It's fascinating to walk down a Japanese street and see English words every now and then on store signs and billboards. None of this stopped Michael, so *Ishido* it was. The complete title was *Ishido, the Way of Stones*.

The Vice President of Product Development at Epyx was Joe Miller, a terrific guy, whose word you could always depend on. I knew from the first moment Michael introduced us that we were going to get along, that I could trust him. Trust is critical when licensing a product to a publisher; a written contract isn't worth all that much.

❧

Joe's first order of business was to determine if we had the people we needed to complete *Ishido*. I had already targeted Mike

Sandige to do the PC version, and Michael Feinberg and Brodie Lockard would do the different game boards and tile sets. I wanted a young programmer, Ian Gilman, from Winslow, Bainbridge Island, Washington to do the Mac. We wanted the Mac to be the lead version; then we would convert it to the PC. At this time in the history of computer games, this kind of product worked best in a menu-based, graphical interface environment, in other words, the Macintosh. Joe was very concerned that our Mac programmer be up to snuff.

I became acquainted with Ian when he sent me a copy of a game he had done called *LineDriver*. This was one of a handful of "living room" products that was worth a close look. Ian was fifteen or sixteen at the time. I was impressed and told him I would love to use him on a project should the opportunity arise. He thought that was a great idea. Now it looked like *Ishido* was just the ticket.

Joe wasn't convinced, "From what you tell me, Ian's just a kid. Do you even know how old he is?"

I shook my head and said, "I'm not sure, but I've met him and I'm confident he can do the job."

"I know your background, and I'm sure that you're a good judge of talent. But this is a critical program for us and we must be sure. We're going to have to interview him."

It seemed I was always up against this "experience needed" mentality. It didn't matter that my products had always shipped. Or that most of my programs were completed on time. Publishers insisted on second guessing my choices in professional talent. I tended to evaluate attitude higher than experience. I used my intuition more than the observable facts (professed experience base). They didn't understand this. They needed proof. It wouldn't matter so much if their methods worked better, but they don't. Extremely late projects and "vaporware" (projects that never ship) still continue to be very common in the industry. There's not a company immune.

So now I had to find a way to get Ian down to the San Francisco Bay Area from Seattle. This may seem like a simple thing, but it wasn't. First, I perceived a problem with time off from school or his parent's potential concern about his making the trip on short notice. In addition, the expenses would run us well over a thousand dollars. Not only wasn't this expense budgeted; this was happening at a time when our cash flow was essentially nonexistent. I had a problem.

I called Ian, told him that Epyx was willing to consider him for the project, "But they insist on evaluating your professional skills. This means we have to find a way to get you down here for the technical interview."

"That's not a problem," he said. "My girlfriend just won a trip to San Francisco on the radio. We're coming down next Friday. Will that work?"

Boy, I love it when there are angels on my side!

Was this serendipity or synchronicity? I'd vote for synchronicity. The goal was to get Ian down to San Francisco and that goal was reached, not a different one. However, it took a coincidence beyond comprehension, a very meaningful coincidence (a small miracle), to make it happen—that's synchronicity. Whatever, we *seized the moment!*

Ian's interview went great and Joe said they'd okay him for the project. That night Kathie and I took Ian and his girlfriend out to dinner to celebrate.

Ian was a tall, gangly, but handsome kid with a look about him that felt much older than his seventeen years. He was a great conversationalist, with a breadth of knowledge that was surprising. His parents were very well-known leaders in the sustainable living movement and publishers of an excellent environmental newsletter/magazine, *In Context.* It was a lovely dinner, a chance for everyone to get to know each other better. We also discovered we still liked each other. This helps when you're going to be working together on a significant project.

Near the end of the meal, it dawned on me that Ian was just seventeen. I should say, the fact of that finally rose to my consciousness.

"Ian, this project isn't going to interrupt your schooling, is it?" I asked.

"Oh, I don't go to school," he responded.

"Did you graduate early?"

"No, I've gotten my GED, but it won't be official until I'm eighteen."

"Did you drop out of high school?"

"Actually, I never went to high school."

Never went to high school! What's going on here? I decided to pursue it. "You dropped out of Junior High?"

"Well, actually, I didn't go to Junior High either."

"When did you drop out?"

"During the fourth grade."

"Oh, I get it. You were home schooled," I said with conviction.

"Not really."

"All right, I'm through with this guessing game. Just tell me what happened."

"I got bored during the fourth grade, so I told my parents I wanted them to go to school and tell the teachers how to teach me. They asked if I thought I could do a better job myself. I said, 'Yes.' And that was that. From then on I've been responsible for my own education."

I was incredulous.

"You mean they trusted you to learn what you needed to learn all on your own?"

"Basically. There was one commitment I had to make." I motioned for him to continue. "I had to commit to spend at least one day a week at the local library."

"Just one day a week?" I asked. This was interesting. I was very curious.

"Yep," he responded.

"What happened? Did it work?"

"Not the first year. It was pretty much a waste of time. But after that I started to get interested in the books. Actually, I've read every book in the library. Of course, I've ended up going well beyond the library in areas I have strong interest…like computers for instance."

"Did you miss not going to school? I mean…friends, social interaction…things like that?"

"Not really, I belong to a local theater club. Year before last we did a tour of Russia, performing our plays in many different towns and cities. The one thing I missed was not having a lab. There were things, for instance, biology or chemistry, where having a lab would have helped. But that's really it."

All of this was a great surprise to me. Somehow I had thought that Abraham Lincoln was the last self-taught person in America. A vision of Ian laying on the floor, reading a book by the light of the fire, jumped into my mind. I'm continually amazed at how much goes on in the world that I have no knowledge about.

* * *

The next day I took Ian aside and gave him a copy of the *Ishido* design document. We spent a couple of minutes discussing the game and how it should play, and then I said, "Now, and listen to me carefully, I don't want you to begin programming until I have received a commitment from Epyx. Commitment means money, so until I have the initial payment, I don't want you to do anything. Understand?"

"Sure. But I might play around with it a little. I'd like to get a feeling for how difficult it's going to be."

I was afraid of this. Youthful exuberance is almost impossible to contain.

"Look, understand this, if they cancel the project, I won't be able to pay you a penny. Got it?"

"Oh, don't worry, that makes sense to me."

And that ended our conversation.

A week later, I was in Joe Miller's office and he was saying, "You know how long it takes to complete a contract." This was rhetorical, but I nodded my head anyway. He continued, "We've agreed on all the major points. We're going to do a contract. I want *Ishido* in time for Christmas. What if I give you enough to get started, say…fifty thousand dollars. Could you get started right away?"

"You hand me a check for fifty thousand dollars and I begin immediately. Do it soon, and I'll promise the product in time for Christmas," I responded with confidence.

He picked an envelop up off the top of his desk and handed it to me, saying, "Get to work…and I want to see a first playable in thirty days."

I called Ian as soon as I got home. "I've got good news and bad news. The good news is we can start the project; I got the first payment. The bad news is, they want to see a first playable in thirty days. What's the chance of that happening?"

"Well, I'm playing it already."

A short conversation, a simple design document, and one week later he's already got first playable. This wasn't possible. I was concerned to say the least.

I didn't need to worry. The first playable was perfect. I held on to it for a couple of weeks before giving it to Joe. I didn't want to breed any unusual expectations.

Development on *Ishido* continued like this, trouble free and easy as pie. It felt like nothing could go wrong. Ian was adding features to the program that made it much more than I ever imagined, and Michael had designed in an oracle, based on the I Ching, that was fabulous. I Ching masters have told us that the I Ching in *Ishido* is the best computer version ever done.

Ishido was turning into the masterpiece I had foreseen when Michael first brought it to me. There was no doubt in my mind that people would still be playing it a thousand years from now.

Protecting Our Rights

About half way into the development of *Ishido*, Joe called me and asked if I could come to his office for a quick meeting. When I arrived he didn't look happy, and I was afraid that something terrible had gone wrong.

He got right to the point, "Brad, the company is having some financial difficulties. We want to continue development of *Ishido*, but to be honest, I'm not sure how much longer we can continue paying the milestones."

"Are you having a hard time telling me that you want to cancel the project?" I asked.

"No, exactly the opposite in fact. What I'm trying to say is that we believe *Ishido* is our best chance to solve our financial problems. We're just not sure that we're going to have enough money to finish the project. I'm wondering how you feel about that?" He was speaking very carefully, almost like he was afraid of my answer.

"It's a scary proposition for me," I answered. "Depending on a lot of things, we might consider finishing the Mac, but I sure wouldn't want to finish the PC version. The risk would be too great."

"You said, 'Depending on a lot of things...,' What kinds of things?"

"Most important is how close are you to bankruptcy? And second, how is this going to impact your ability to market the product effectively?"

These were critical issues for me, so critical that I had insisted that both be part of the written contract. According to the contract, we got the rights to *Ishido* back if they could no longer market the product effectively. While what was needed for this to happen was open to interpretation, we also got the rights back the instant they filed for bankruptcy.

"I don't believe we are anywhere near bankruptcy. And we are focusing on our marketing, because we know how critical that effort is, as we work our way out of this situation," Joe responded.

"Boy, this is a tough business," I said with a high level of frustration.

"I considered waiting until things got worse before saying anything," Joe said. "But I wanted to give you some warning. I'd hoped you might be able to plan your budget so that you could continue development should we run into trouble and possibly end up late on a milestone payment."

"I appreciate the advance notice. I'll discuss it with Dick and we'll see what we can do. In the meantime, please keep me informed."

"That I promise," he said, and I got up and left.

Joe kept his promise about keeping me informed, but things only went from bad to worse. Then about a month later, he called me.

"Brad, I just wanted you to know that I'm leaving." he said.

"What do you mean, you're leaving? You're my only contact with Epyx. What's going on?" I said with panic in my voice.

"Not very much good, I'm afraid. We've laid off the entire marketing department, and we're filing for bankruptcy this afternoon. We're filing for reorganization but, to be honest with you, I don't see much hope. I've recommended that we return the rights to *Ishido* to you immediately."

"I get the rights back as soon as you file; that's clear in the contract. In addition, I get the rights back when you are no longer able to market the product. I would say that laying off the entire marketing department meets that requirement."

"Between you and me, I wouldn't bet on it. Our major stockholder, Tom Wezzel, is taking over the company during reorganization, and at the last management meeting he told us that he intends on keeping the rights to *Ishido*. He said the lawyers have assured him they can get the bankruptcy judge to throw out the contract."

"Throw out the contract? I don't understand." I was very confused.

"That's what I said. If they can prove that *Ishido* is essential to the reorganization, the judge will rule the section of the contract relating to the return of rights as invalid, and Epyx will retain the rights, regardless of what the contract says."

"But how can they prove that? The product isn't even completed. It's worthless to Epyx as it is, and there's no way we would finish it under the circumstances. The best thing would be to give us the rights back, let us license *Ishido* to someone else, and then pay back the money you've advanced us. That would give your creditors $125,000. If they do what you say, the creditors won't get a thing. "

"I agree, that's why I'm recommending that we return the rights to you. But Tom doesn't see it that way; and, well, let's just say he can be stubborn at times."

It worked out just like Joe had figured it would. The judge made the decision based on what he was told by Epyx's attorneys. We didn't even get to present our side of the case. *Ishido* was literally stolen from us, with no regard for the written contract and complete ignorance concerning the actual situation.

It didn't appear that we could do anything about it. Nobody would license *Ishido* with this "legal" cloud hanging over it, and we couldn't even consider fighting the ruling. When I checked into this, I was told the minimum it would cost us was $50,000, and the legal fees could run over $100,000.

The worst part was that it wouldn't cost Epyx anything to fight us. All of their legal fees would come from money that was earmarked for the creditors, because the court had identified *Ishido* as essential to the reorganization. We were stuck.

I'd heard it before, that the courts were incapable of making educated, intelligent decisions when it came to the computer industry. I'm sure there are instances where the courts do a good job, but *Ishido* wasn't one of them. Nobody was going to win here, not Publishing International, not Epyx, and especially not Epyx's creditors. Oh, I forgot...of course, there would be winners—the lawyers. It sounds like an old joke, but it wasn't funny.

It was still important that we finish the Macintosh version. We had retained the Asian rights and secured the services of Jan Putnam, JP International, to represent us in Japan. Jan, even though a woman working in the extremely male Japanese business environment, was the best computer games agent in Japan. She was anxious to begin showing *Ishido* around, but needed the final Mac version before the major Japanese publishers would look at it.

I discovered what a committed team I had. Everyone agreed to continue with the Mac version until it was finished. They accepted that we would pay what we could during development, and would pay the rest once we had successfully licensed it to a Japanese software publisher. It felt very good to know how trusted we were.

Finally it was done, and we were ready to send it out to the major Japanese publishers.

"This is only the first step, Brad. If they like it, we'll have to go to Japan to do the final negotiations. Are you prepared for that?" Jan asked.

"I guess so. I sure haven't had any trouble working with the Fujitsu people," I responded.

"The Fujitsu people are the most conservative. If you're able to work with them, you should be able to work with everyone else."

It didn't take long before we received the initial responses. They were beyond all of our expectations. What I didn't know then, was how popular *Shanghai* was in Japan. It had been a smash hit; everyone played it. It was on computers, game machines, even in the arcades; it was the number one game in all of Japan.

And in Japan it's the producer who is often the star. When the publishers discovered that the producer for *Ishido* (another compelling tile game, very much like *Shanghai*) had been the producer for *Shanghai*...well, that sealed it; I had to go to Japan.

This was literally the first time I had been in a foreign country (not including Canada, and Tijuana, Mexico). I was fascinated by the differences between Japan and the United States, as well as affirmed by the ways we were alike.

I was surprised to see that they drive on the other side of the street. They walk on the other side too. I hadn't expected that. And the way they determine a company's street address is curious—not in the order they appear on the street—but rather, in the order that they were originally built. This is not the place to be a postman or cab driver.

I loved the food in Japan (except for the Chinese food), and I loved having a McDonalds near my hotel. Twice I got up in the middle of the night to go and get a hamburger, as much for something familiar, as to quiet my hunger.

Finally, I loved doing business with the Japanese. They were gracious, understanding, and honorable. All in all, it was a terrific experience, as well as being financially rewarding. We had no trouble paying the *Ishido* team what we owed them when I got back. Thank God I had insisted on retaining the Asian rights. That decision ended up saving our company.

Fujitsu Limited licensed the FM Towns version of *Ishido* while we were in Japan. This would be the second product (*Solitaire Royale* was first) we would be doing for them.

During development it became obvious that *Ishido*, like *Solitaire Royale*, would take up a very small percentage of the available space on the CDROM (all Fujitsu product was distributed on CDROM). This time I was determined to fill it up.

Ishido is kind of a mystical game, definitely one of the "meditative strategy" genre. I thought it would be terrific if we could include some "new age" type music with it, meditative music coordinated to different themes found in the game, that could be listened to while playing the game. Additionally, adding fifty minutes of original music would fill up the CDROM nicely. I called Ed Bogas.

"Ed, I need fifty minutes of original music for a game I'm doing for Fujitsu Limited in Japan. Can you help me?"

"I've got a recording session next Tuesday...I can squeeze you in then. Will that work?" he asked.

"Great! When can we get together and discuss it? I'll need about ten original pieces, and I have specific themes in mind for each of them."

"Bring your list with you; we'll do it on the fly."

"What do you mean, do it on the fly?" This didn't sound right.

"I'll improvise according to your themes. It shouldn't be a problem. I'll have a couple of hours." He said this with great confidence.

"I was hoping for a live orchestra. That was the feeling I was looking for."

"Of course," he said.

"Ed, are you telling me that you will create fifty minutes of original music, ten different songs, written to match the themes that I have planned. Then you'll perform and record this new music using a full orchestra, finally handing me the completed tape...and the whole thing, from start to finish will take two hours?" I said incredulously.

"Sure, that's plenty of time...trust me."

"This I've got to see."

I'm not going to try and tell you what happened during that recording session. But not much more than two hours after entering the studio, I walked out with the final tape of the music, ready to be added to the *Ishido* CDROM. And the music was so good it was released as a separate album in Japan.

When I got back from Japan I was greeted with a great surprise. Accolade, the company Al Miller and Bob Whitehead had formed after leaving Activision, wanted to publish *Ishido* and, wonder of wonders, was willing to front us the legal costs so we could get the rights back. We would have to pay them back, but we could do it out of our royalties. This was good news indeed.

The word about our success in Japan had gotten back to Accolade, and they were determined to have the rights to sell *Ishido* in America and the rest of the world. I was delighted. We not only had the funds to fight Tom Wezzel and Epyx; I was also going to be able to work with Al Miller again. I looked forward to that.

We chose to use Accolade's law firm, and it seemed to me that we should be able to solve this problem relatively quickly. It was obvious that Epyx was not going to be able to market *Ishido*. While they believed they had rights to it, there was nothing anyone could do to force us to finish it for them. It turned out they never told the judge that *Ishido* wasn't finished. They never could have gotten him to assign rights to them if they had.

After a promising start, Accolade's law firm basically accomplished nothing. It seemed to me all they ever did was have meetings and discuss the situation. The only action taken was a couple of letters to Epyx, and they were effectively ignored. Two months into the project and we were out thousands of dollars, but basically we were no better off than when we had started.

I decided to take matters into my own hands. I contacted another law office recommended by a friend. I was assigned a woman attorney, Laura Rafaty, who turned out to be our guardian angel. Laura was appalled at the situation. She couldn't believe the courts and the legal process could have treated us so badly, and she was determined to right what she saw as a terrible wrong.

She immediately began the process of taking depositions from all of the major players: myself, Dick, Joe Miller, and, of course, Tom Wezzel.

I remember clearly the drive to San Francisco from our offices in Sunnyvale when I was on my way to give my deposition. I was listening to the program *Fresh Air* on the local public radio station, and they were doing a segment on a new book about the top Mafia leader in the United States.

The interviewer, Terry Gross, was surprised that the author had been so candid in the book, including providing a list of "competitors" that the Mafia leader had had "eliminated."

"Aren't you afraid that you're next? After all, you've pointed the finger right at him," she said.

"Why should I be afraid? He was aware that I was writing this book, what I was going to say in it," the author responded.

"I don't understand. He let you say all of these terrible things about him...how were you able to pull that one off?"

"First, I let it be known that I wanted to write the book. Some individuals came to me and asked what I wanted to write about, what I planned on saying. I was honest with them. They went away. Then I heard that it had been okayed, and others came forward with the information and stories that I have in the book."

"Why would he give his permission? And, what if he changes his mind and gets mad at you, once he sees it in print?" she asked.

"First, remember, even though you and I think what he did was terrible, he's proud of it. He set a goal to become the top Mafia leader in the United States. He knew what he would have to do to accomplish that goal. He wants the world to know what he accomplished, and how he did it. In this way he's no different than you and me.

"As far as changing his mind and coming after me, it won't happen. The Mafia has a strong code of ethics. Once the deal is made, that's it. It's a matter of honor. They don't need lawyers to enforce their contracts. Anyone who doesn't live up to their word finds themselves standing on the bottom of the Hudson river in a pair of cement overshoes. No, I don't have to worry."

It's a matter of honor...I couldn't help but think how I'd much rather do business with the Mafia than Tom Wezzel and Epyx. Then I had a vision of Tom standing on the bottom of San Francisco Bay in a pair of cement overshoes. I couldn't help but laugh out loud.

━━━━⋄━━━━

The depositions supported our position. It seemed like a no brainer. Laura talked with Epyx's attorney and determined that she, too, agreed that this was just costing everyone a lot of money. The facts were in, and it was ridiculous to continue with the contention that the rights to *Ishido* belonged to Epyx.

Tom proved to be much worse than "a bit stubborn sometimes." He proved to be a selfish, ignorant jerk who was only interested in causing trouble, especially if it wasn't costing him any money. We were forced to bare the additional cost of going to court.

The actual court case was very anti-climatic. After about five minutes, the judge (not the same one who made the initial ruling) effectively told us to get out of there and not bother him with such obvious cases.

"Do what the contract says for God's sake!" And that was that.

It ended up costing us $75,000 to get the court to tell us to do exactly what I had wanted to do from the beginning. It cost the creditors at Epyx approximately the same amount. In addition, I had to return the $125,000 that Epyx had advanced us. Cement overshoes would have been so much more cost effective and easier. It's no wonder that American business and the court system have such a bad reputation.

***

With the Japanese contracts, we ended up making money on *Ishido*, but it never became the big winner that *Shanghai* had been, never generated millions of dollars in revenue for us and our publishers. It had a lot of incarnations here in America, as well as winning many major awards.

We, Publishing International, published a limited edition version sold in a beautiful wooden box that could be displayed on a coffee table. This version was awarded five stars by MacUser magazine, one of the few games ever to gain that honor.

The versions published by Accolade also won many awards, and *Ishido* had the highest customer satisfaction rating of any game that Accolade ever sold. This proved to us, that once somebody tried it, they loved it. Accolade just couldn't figure out how to get the word out to everyone.

A few years after Accolade had finished with *Ishido*, and the rights had once again returned to Publishing International, I got a call from Phil Adam, who was now with Interplay Productions.

"Brad, we're starting a new line of games for the Macintosh and we want *Ishido*. What's the chance?"

"Pretty good. When do you want it?" I asked.

"How soon can you get it to us?" he asked.

"Tomorrow soon enough?"

This would be the third American publisher for the Macintosh version of *Ishido*. A few thousand more people would discover it, spend many enjoyable hours playing it.

If *Ishido* is destined to being played a thousand years from now, it will be like an artist's masterpiece, achieving true fame after the artist and the producer are dead and in their graves.

For some there is a sadness in this thought. But I suspect the artist, if he could have known that his pictures would be enjoyed by millions after he was gone, would have found great joy in that knowledge. After all, the true artist creates for the sake of creating. That others may ultimately find something of value in his work is a bonus that is often not received and is only contemplated in his most optimistic moments.

Ishido was given to Michael as a gift from a source we don't yet understand...then he gifted it to me. Finally, through the efforts of many and in spite of numerous difficulties, we gifted it to the world, to those who on discovering it, spent many hours pleasured by its beauty, challenged by the game, and awed by its oracle. This is enough for me.

So Close Chapter 20

Card solitaire was one of our first products. And I am continually amazed at its world-wide acceptance.

It wasn't long after I completed *Solitaire Royale* that Microsoft Windows was released with a card solitaire game included. Lots of people assumed it was a version of our product. I only wish that it had been. What wouldn't I have given to have a demo of *Solitaire Royale* shipped with Windows? This is the independent software developer's dream.

In September of 1991, I was at a Software Publishers' Association (SPA) conference in Orlando, Florida, when I was approached by two guys I had never met before.

"Brad, I'm Tom Wright, and this is Bill Young. We're from Microsoft. We'd like to buy you a cup of coffee."

"I don't drink coffee, but I'll have an iced tea with you," I replied.

We made our way to the coffee shop in the hotel without saying much of anything. They were sizing me up, and I was trying to figure out what these guys from Microsoft wanted with me.

"I suppose you're wondering what this is all about?" Tom asked.

"That hits the nail on the head," I replied.

"Basically, it's about card solitaire," he said. "Have you seen the version of it we shipped with Windows?

"Are you kidding?"

He ignored my question and went on. "I'm not afraid to tell you that it was inspired by *Solitaire Royale*. You did a terrific job."

"Thank you," I replied. "I suspected someone up there had seen *Solitaire Royale*. It's nice of you to confirm that."

I couldn't help but think that this was the second product of mine Microsoft had copied. I was tempted to make a remark to that effect but decided to keep it to myself. Instead I said, "Is this iced tea my official thanks for bringing computer card solitaire to the world?"

"Why don't I quit playing around and tell you what we have in mind," Tom said as he glanced toward Bill.

I made an affirming gesture and he continued.

"We've noticed that the single most commented on, most used feature of Microsoft Windows is the solitaire game. It's hard to walk down a hallway without seeing a number of people playing it. This isn't just true at Microsoft; we're finding it true at companies all over the world."

He stopped to see if I wanted to add anything; I didn't, so he went on.

"On top of that, we haven't seen a review of Microsoft Windows that didn't favorably comment on solitaire." He paused considering his next words carefully.

"What we're thinking is we've got the world's most successful demo, but we don't have the product."

"You can say that again," I replied with a hint of laughter.

"Would you consider doing *Microsoft Solitaire*?" he asked.

I wasn't sure I'd heard him right, "Are you saying you want to talk to me about designing and developing a computer card solitaire product for Microsoft?" I asked.

"That's what we're saying." Tom replied.

This was extremely appealing to me. Spectrum Holobyte's focus on doing simulations for the military had impacted *Soli-*

taire Royale as well as a number of other products of ours. This meant I needed a new home for solitaire. I had, in fact, prepared a design specification for a new card solitaire product called *Solitaire Challenge* that I was planning on shopping around. What could be better than to have that home be Microsoft, the best marketing company in the world?

"You've got my attention. How do we go about making this happen?" I asked.

"We need to discuss our plans more completely, and you will have to sign some necessary paperwork before we can proceed. Can you come up to Microsoft and visit with us?" Tom asked.

"You name the date," I responded.

"We're going to be busy for the next few weeks with Comdex. How about sometime during the last couple of weeks in October?"

"I can make that work," I responded. "Will we be discussing the contract at that time too?"

"If everything else works out, we should be able to enter contract negotiations soon after that. The contract process at Microsoft is a rigorous one. I hope you're prepared for it."

"I don't think you could be any tougher than Fujitsu. They're a wonderful company to work with, but it takes months to get through the contract process with them."

"Ours isn't any worse, might even be a little better. I'm hoping things will work out, and we can sign well before the next SPA meeting six months from now. It's important to Bill and me that this product be ready for the holiday season."

"That shouldn't be a problem," I said. "It isn't like we haven't done a card solitaire game before. This has turned out to be quite a meeting; thank you for this opportunity."

For the next week and a half, I was as excited as a guy who just found out he won the lottery. It looked like I had, since the royalties for *Microsoft Solitaire* would be in the millions of dollars. I had no doubt this would be one of their most successful products. Like Tom had said, "...we've got the world's most successful demo..." and now *we* would be doing the game! This was the opportunity of a lifetime.

They started the meeting at Microsoft by showing me a new game they had just added to their Entertainment Pak. "…it's called *Stones*," Tom said.

"This is a copy of my game *Ishido*," I said.

Conversation stopped as I played it for a moment. Everyone was embarrassed. They were embarrassed for being caught, not knowing that I had been the developer of *Ishido*; and I was embarrassed because I was up there to convince them I was the right guy to do *Microsoft Solitaire*, and here I was accusing them of ripping me off.

But it was disconcerting. This was the third product of mine that Microsoft had copied. While I didn't feel I had any rights to the playing of card solitaire on the computer (that was public domain), the copying of *Shanghai* and *Ishido* was a completely different matter.

The silence as I played the game was deafening.

Finally Tom felt uncomfortable enough to say something. "Do you want me to check into it?"

By that time I had played the game and discovered that the programmer, in his attempt to change the rules enough to avoid charges of copyright infringement, had completely destroyed the game play.

"No, it's not necessary."

Tom was relieved. He had begun to think there might be a problem, and now it seemed to have gone away.

"Well then, let's start discussing solitaire," he said.

Their process turned out to be rigorous, and when it didn't look like they were going to be finished in time for us to have a product ready by the holiday season, Tom called me, "Brad, I have to have this. What if we send you a very strong letter of intent, one that guarantees that we will do the product as long as all the major contractual issues are met? Could you begin development right away?"

"I don't know, Tom, that's a big risk on our part," I replied. "We're a small development company. We will have to borrow money to get the project started. If anything happened, we couldn't afford it. It could even bankrupt us."

"I know it's risky, but it's important to you too. Think how much you'll make if we release it this year." He was tempting me.

"Send me your letter. We'll take a look at it, and if it makes sense, we'll go ahead and start."

The letter was very strong. There was no doubt they were committed, so we started the project.

As it turned out the negotiations took the entire six months. But finally everything was done, just in time for the next SPA meeting, which, coincidentally was being held in Seattle. Tom called just before the meeting to tell me he had gotten the final signoffs on the contract, including Bill Gates, and that we could have the signing and celebration when I was up there.

I could hardly believe it was true. It wasn't. Tom was difficult to reach when I arrived. I finally found him at a Microsoft event held especially for SPA members.

"Tom, what's going on? I thought you'd be looking for me. Don't we have a contract to sign?

"Something's come up, and we won't be able to sign right now," he said. "I thought I'd fly down and see you next week. Okay?"

I said it was okay, but I knew in my heart it wasn't. I knew something real bad was about to happen. I was right...we never heard from Microsoft again. This is the absolute truth. They not only didn't explain what happened, they never even called to tell us that the deal was off. In all my years, before and since, I have never been treated so poorly.

This was a devastating blow for us and came close to driving us into bankruptcy. I called and called, but none of my calls were returned. It was like Tom had dropped off the face of the planet.

In desperation I wrote a long personal letter to Bill Gates. My aunt and uncle were personal friends of Bill's mother and father. They were in the same bridge club together, had been for years. I thought with this strong personal connection, I'd at least get an answer, an explanation. In my letter I explained the entire situation, including our personal connection. We sent the letter registered mail and received confirmation that it had been received by Microsoft. As I stated earlier, we never heard back. We no longer existed as a company as far as Microsoft was concerned.

I did discover what happened. A business acquaintance of mine had just been hired into their games division. I called and asked him to look into the matter.

He called back and told me Tom had been reassigned, and another guy had come in to run the games division. When the new guy got there and discovered they were about to sign a contract for computer solitaire, he said, "I don't want to do a stupid solitaire game!" and he tossed the contract into the wastebasket. My friend said Tom was sorry it had happened, but he couldn't do anything about it.

What do you do when something this devastating happens to you? How do you bounce back? How do you move on when your dreams have been so thoroughly shattered; your opportunity for financial independence taken away by the whim of an arrogant, ignorant, insensitive jerk; your company's entire future threatened, with no more concern than a horse has for the flies buzzing around it's tail?

We considered suing Microsoft, but I didn't like that idea. There was the problem of money for lawyers and court costs; but with the letter we had, it wouldn't have been too hard to find an attorney to work on spec. It isn't often you get a chance to sue Microsoft with a good chance of winning. But I'd already discovered the hard way that lawsuits take all of your time and energy, and they focus on the past. I like to live in the present.

I decided to forget Microsoft and try to place *Solitaire for Windows* with another publisher. It wouldn't mean anywhere near the same success financially, but in order to be prepared to *seize the moment*, you need to drive forward looking out the windshield, instead of backward looking through the rear-view mirror.

Phil Adam had become a VP for Interplay Productions; and when he discovered that *Solitaire* was available again, he jumped on it. That's how they came to publish *Solitaire for Windows* and it's sequel, *Solitaire Deluxe.*

It was ten years later, as I was sharing with some people from the games division at Microsoft how I had almost done a card solitaire product for them, that one of the executives said, "You know our research has told us that card solitaire is the most played game in the world."

"You should know," I said. "You've got the most successful demo of all time."

"But we still don't have the game!" he said. And everyone laughed.

The Microsoft Myth Chapter 21

When a company has hurt you as much as I have been hurt by Microsoft, if you attack them in any way, people assume that you're just angry or out to get them. So you end up being quiet about it.

In business, just as with test pilots, there's a "right stuff" attitude. The belief is if you win, you had the "right stuff." If you lose, you didn't.

Gary Kildall of Digital Research put it like this, "The winner of the battle, not the loser, gets their version recorded as history."

What this means is that a company like Microsoft has very few critics. Their real critics are the competitors that have been threatened or defeated; they can't say anything. While their friends, the ones making money because of Microsoft, won't say anything.

I think it's time somebody said something. Somehow I feel like a kid yelling at the top of my lungs, **"But, mommy, he doesn't have any clothes on!"**

> *"We are going to succeed in maintaining our right to innovate...if you take it as a given that we are going to be blocked from innovating...this would jump to the top of [reasons] why Microsoft will go out of business soon."*
> Bill Gates,
> *Newsweek* Magazine,
> March 9th, 1998.

This is the Microsoft myth. *The belief that Microsoft is an innovative company.*

Let's give credit where credit is due. Bill Gates is the smartest marketing genius in the world today, probably ever. Microsoft knows how to do business and how to do it well. But they are not, nor have they ever been, innovators. Microsoft has never had an original idea in it's history; or, if they have had one, it's never seen the light of day.

This goes back at least as far at the "development" of MS-DOS, the product upon which the Microsoft world-wide computer system monopoly is built.

A quick definition here: MS–DOS, Microsoft (MS) Disk Operating System (DOS). It is the DOS (Disk Operating System) that makes it possible for a computer to work; without DOS there wouldn't be any way people could communicate with computers. A computer without DOS is like a telephone without a speaker.

It is also common knowledge that Bill Gates bought MS-DOS from Tim Patterson at Seattle Computer Products for a flat fee, in the neighborhood of $50,000.

It is remarkable how much MS-DOS looked, felt, and

worked like the beta version of a new DOS, DR–DOS, from Digital Research in Monterey California. (For you purists, it wasn't called DR–DOS at this time, I think it was called CPM-86.) When asked about this, Tim says, "I didn't copy anything. I just took their printed documentation and did something that did the same thing." However, it is also a fact that both Seattle Computer Products and Microsoft had copies of the beta version of the new Digital Research DOS (opportunity). And it is known that IBM needed a disk operating system for it's new personal computer badly, and Bill was willing to deal with them in a way that Digital Research didn't seem to be willing to (motivation).

The legend in the Silicon Valley is that MS-DOS was a total rip-off of Digital's beta, but when Gary Kildall threatened to sue Microsoft and IBM, he was told by an IBM executive, "Go ahead, we have better lawyers and more money. You haven't got a chance."

Even without this legendary threat, Gary definitely had a problem. Copyright laws regarding software were very nebulous at that time. I'm sure Gary's legal advisors would have told him there was no way of determining the outcome; there was a good chance he could spend his fortune and lose the battle. We will never know for sure what happened. Gary is dead (he died in an accident a couple of years ago), and Bill has already created his version of history.

The result was that the market place had two versions of DOS from the very beginning, MS–DOS and DR–DOS. They both worked identically, but because IBM controlled the PC market on the DOS side in those early years, other manufacturers felt it was important to use the same DOS that IBM was using. So in the U.S. we were hardly aware of DR–DOS.

Personally, I preferred DR–DOS for two reasons: firstly, because I like to support the underdog and secondly, because it had less bugs and crashed less often. They both ran all of the same programs equally as well...what a coincidence.

Let's look at another significant Microsoft product, Windows. Again, it's common knowledge that the original Windows was remarkably like the Macintosh. I remember when I was invited up to Microsoft by my good friend and previous boss at Activision, Tom Lopez.

After leaving Activision, Tom spent a year developing an extremely innovative product that put all of the most important reference books on a CDROM and then integrated it so the information would be immediately available to anyone using the computer. The program, *BookShelf*, was an outstanding example of innovation, and Bill Gates immediately saw its potential. Microsoft bought it and Tom became their Vice President of CDROM technology.

It was after all this had happened that I was sitting in Tom's office and he asked, "Do you want to see Microsoft Windows?"

Of course, I did. Rumors had been rampant in the industry that Microsoft was getting ready to introduce this new, revolutionary product. Did I want an advance look at it?

"You bet!" I said.

Tom invited me to sit in the driver's seat (computer lingo for the chair in front of the computer) and he brought up Windows.

"Tom." I said. "It looks just like the Macintosh."

"No, Brad, it's Windows," he replied.

"Tom, it looks just like the Macintosh."

He was silent for a second, and then he looked at me and said, "It's running on a PC."

I couldn't believe how blatant the copying was. It was beyond comprehension. I couldn't understand how Microsoft could let this happen. Surely someone in the organization would have waved a red flag.

Then I read, *Barbarians Lead by Bill Gates* by Jennifer Edstrom and Marlin Eller, and discovered the answer. Marlin was the lead developer for graphics on Windows, an insider who knows what was going on during its development.

At the same time they were developing Windows, they made an agreement with Apple to develop applications for their new computer, the Macintosh. The agreement specified they keep everything about the Macintosh secret. In order to accomplish this, they were legally obligated to put the Macintosh applications group behind a locked a door, into what's called a clean room. Nothing about the Macintosh was to be shared with the rest of the company.

It didn't work out that way. The quote below, from *Barbarians Lead by Bill Gates*, relates to the development of Windows and Bill Gates concerns about how it was coming along.

> "...behind one of the locked doors was a machine (beta version of the Macintosh) from Apple..., Gates was always complaining, 'Why isn't this like the Mac?' and 'Be more like the Mac,' long before the Mac even shipped. This was the mantra that would become numbingly familiar in the months ahead."

That had been Gates plan from the beginning...make Windows just like the Macintosh. It seems it didn't matter to him what they had to do to accomplish this; as far as he was concerned, the ends justified the means.

———

This lack of innovation even went beyond Microsoft's product development. Here's another quote from *Barbarians Lead by Bill Gates*,

"He left his office and walked down the corridor to the center of building 9. All the buildings at Microsoft were shaped like an *X*. Supply rooms, mail rooms, and cafeterias were all in the center of the *X*. *Microsoft had adopted the building design from IBM.*"

They had even copied the design of their buildings!

Here's a simple definition from Webster's New Collegiate:

"Innovation: the introduction of something new, a new idea, method, or device."

To paraphrase a recent presidential candidate, "I know innovators, Bill and...you aren't an innovator."

That's enough of this. Let's get back to the good stuff!

Making Beautiful Music

Michael Feinberg was inspired by the personal success he had achieved through the licensing of *Ishido* into the Japanese market, and he was ready to design a new game, something even more wonderful. He came to me on a clear, crisp February afternoon in 1990.

"Brad, let's do the finest 'meditative strategy' program the world will ever see," he said with eyes blazing.

"Okay, what do you have in mind?" I asked.

"I want it to be everything to everyone. I want gorgeous graphics, a wonderful new game, and the most fantastic puzzles that have ever existed. I already have a name for it...*Heaven & Earth*."

I never knew quite what to say when Michael talked like this. Part of me was always tempted to be the spoiler (I can do that very well, as some of my friends will attest to). But when he looked at me, I felt his vision filling my soul. I was immediately committed to bringing it to fruition. I knew it would happen, and I wanted to be a part of it.

At the same time as Michael was talking about *Heaven & Earth*, I was getting anxious to do another music creativity program with Ed Bogas. We had been talking about music creativity for a few years. He had actually done one program for Broderbund called *Jam Session*. It was for the Macintosh and had received modest success.

I had also done a music creativity program called *The Music Studio* when I was at Activision. The developers for *The Music Studio* had been Rick Parfitt, Rick Forester, and Greg Hospelhorn.

Both *Jam Session* and *The Music Studio* made "making music" much easier and more fun. But Ed and I both knew we had just touched the surface. We could do an even better job given another chance.

One day we were talking on the phone, "Ed, I just got the shipping version of *Ishido* from Fujitsu. When would be a good time for me to bring it around?"

"Anytime this week. If I'm not at home, I'll be at Russian Hill. You can bring it by there," he responded.

"I've been thinking, Ed, we've been talking about doing a music creativity program for a few years now. If you're interested, I'd like to do a short proposal and shop it around. I'm looking for a new project, so what do you think?"

He didn't say anything for a minute and then, "Well, I'm sort of committed to Broderbund, but it doesn't look like they're going to do anything else with *Jam Session*.... Okay, with one provision, if you do sell the idea to someone, I'm going to have to get a release from Broderbund."

"I'll chance it. I'll write something up that describes in general what it is we're trying to do and bring it with me when I bring your copies of *Ishido*. We've talked about it enough…I think I can get the general idea across."

"See you then," he said, ending the conversation.

It was actually a simple concept. We didn't want to teach people how to play an instrument or the basic elements of music. What we wanted to do was make it possible for someone with limited knowledge and talent to have a whole lot of fun with music. There were only three things needed to have fun with music: melody, lyrics, and chords. That was it. The great part was that a lot of people understood music at this level.

Ed talked about the program as being a "machine" for making music. All you had to do was bring together those three elements: melody, lyrics, and chords and...almost by magic...there was your song. To make it even easier, if the user supplied the melody and the lyrics, we would supply the chords.

I liked the idea of a music machine, so I started calling the program, *Ed Bogas' Music Machine*. Ed agreed, under protest, to my using the name as a working title.

"But it's not shipping with that title," he said.

At the same time, Michael was working feverishly on his version of the *Heaven & Earth* proposal. It was fantastic, true multimedia with music, animations, and a compelling story. When he finished with it, we showed it to every publisher on the planet, including ones with headquarters in Europe and Japan. I was also pushing *Ed Bogas' Music Machine*, but neither were high concept. So both were extremely hard to sell.

I was beginning to lose hope, when I got a call from Tom Randolph. "Satoh San is going to be in San Francisco in a couple of weeks. He specifically asked if you could come by and see him, if you might have some new products to show him."

This was Yoshihiro Satoh, a high level executive with Fujitsu Limited in Japan. (He ultimately became a director with the company.) Fujitsu had licensed *Solitaire Royale*, *Hometown, U.S.A.* and *Ishido*. We heard they had been delighted with the programs. The fact he had asked to meet with me specifically was solid affirmation of that rumor.

I decided that Ed and I would go; Ed would use *Jam Session* to do a simple presentation of how music could be made easy on the computer, and then I would talk to Satoh San about both programs. I would use only my simple, twelve page, written proposal for *Heaven & Earth*.

We started with Ed's demo of *Jam Session*, and then I described *Ed Bogas' Music Machine* in a bit more detail. When it seemed that he had gotten the point, I described what we were trying to do with *Heaven & Earth*. Then I handed him the proposals.

He looked them over quickly and then looked up at me and said, "Tell me, Fregger San, will these products be as wonderful as the other products you have so graciously allowed us to license?"

"Yes, Satoh San," I replied.

"Then we wish to license them also," he said.

I was speechless...I stood, mumbled something that I don't remember but that I hoped reflected my gratitude. He stood with me, a smile on his face, and held out his hand. We shook on it and that was that. He really knew how to *seize the moment*, and we were the beneficiaries. Doing business with Yoshihiro Satoh was truly an honor.

It's still hard to believe what happened on that day. In less than an hour, after a short demo and a couple of short presentations supported by two simple design documents, Satoh San had just committed Fujitsu to fund the development of two major software programs, *Heaven & Earth* and *Ed Bogas' Music Machine*.

But things are never as simple nor as easy as they seem. Satoh San had committed to the projects; we had shaken hands on the deal. However, when the managers in charge of their software development program investigated it, they got very nervous with the amount of money and resources that had been committed. Especially since all I had to show for supporting materials were two simple design scenarios, not even complete design specifications.

We attempted to correct things by producing full design specifications, with Michael and I taking full responsibility for *Heaven & Earth*, and Tom Randolph's company, Lanpro, funding the one for *Ed Bogas' Music Machine*. It didn't help. They wanted to see prototypes on the computer. They felt the risk was too great.

I was devastated when we received what amounted to a rejection letter from Fujitsu. I couldn't believe it. Satoh San had given his personal commitment. This wasn't like them. I wrote Satoh San a letter and faxed it to his office in Tokyo.

"Dear Satoh San…I am, therefore, very confused…I thought we had shaken hands on this deal…that I had your commitment…am I wrong in believing this?"

Two days later I received an overnight delivery from the Fujitsu offices in Tokyo. Included were first drafts of licensing contracts for both *Heaven & Earth* and *Ed Bogas' Music Machine*, plus a letter apologizing for the confusion and reemphasizing their commitment to fund the development of these projects. Satoh San didn't make a commitment and then not keep it.

I couldn't help but remember the fight we had the previous year over *Ishido*. That time we had signed a contract assuring us we would get the rights back if Epyx went into bankruptcy, but it had cost us $75,000 to get a court to agree.

A couple of years later, we had received a strong letter of intent from Microsoft, only to be cancelled without notice and without notification.

Fujitsu honored a simple handshake…and people ask me why I enjoyed doing business with the Japanese!

When you licensed an original product with an American publisher, most often you surrendered world-wide rights for all computer and video game systems. Licensing an original product with Fujitsu was a dream come true. They didn't want world-wide rights. They only asked that you not begin development on a competing Japanese version until after you had shipped the FMTowns version.

This meant we could still license both *Heaven & Earth* and *Ed Bogas' Music Machine* to any other publisher in the world. In addition, with the Fujitsu funding, we were able to produce excellent prototypes within a short period of time. It was even better than that; they loaned me an FMTowns computer, so I could demo the products to other publishers.

Walt Disney Interactive Software licensed *Heaven & Earth* to be the first product for their new Buena Vista Software line. They hoped that the Buena Vista line would become to software what Touchstone meant to movies. Before Touchstone, Disney hadn't been able to market anything but "G" rated movies. As I said earlier, their software division was having the same problem.

The development of *Ed Bogas' Music Machine* was coming along nicely. I had been able to talk Greg Hosplehorn, one of the developers for *The Music Studio*, into being the technical director for the project. He did most of the technical design and the vast majority of the programming. This meant we had the producer and one of the main programmers for the *The Music Studio* and the creator of *Jam Session* doing *Ed Bogas' Music Machine*. I was confident it would be everything we had hoped for.

It was a little more difficult to license it. American publishers couldn't figure out how to market it, weren't sure there even was a market. I never understood this.

Creativity programs, especially in the area of art and graphics, have seen tremendous success. *The Print Shop* was one of Broderbund's biggest sellers. *Coral Draw* also continues to make millions of dollars for its publisher. There are many different graphics programs available to the consumer, at all levels of expertise. But this hasn't been true for music. There are music programs that have experienced some success, and there are some professional programs that make it possible for the user to do anything.

But nothing significant has been done for the person who has average musical talent and skill—the person who loves music, either plays an instrument fairly well or dreams about waking up some morning and being able to—the person who just wants to have fun with music.

It was about this time that I got a call from Stuart Bond at Electronic Arts. He was the senior executive in charge of a big percentage of EA's product development.

"Brad, will you have lunch with me?"

"I'd like that," I answered. "You name the time and the place, and I'll be there."

We ended up eating at a fabulous Chinese restaurant in Menlo Park. We were near the end of lunch when Stuart said, "What are you working on now...anything interesting?"

Ed Bogas' Music Machine was all that I was working on, but conversations around that product had never gone anywhere before. I hesitated to bring it up.

When I didn't answer right away, he said, "You must be working on something. What's the problem? Are you under non-disclosure?"

"No, nothing like that...it's just that I've had so much trouble explaining what we've got that I'd love to license to a major publisher...well, I hesitate to bring it up."

"I'm not your normal guy...give it a try."

I launched into my "speech" about the need for a consumer music creation tool, one that really worked, one that millions would find fun and exciting. Stuart didn't have any trouble following me. In fact, when I had been doing *Music Studio*, he had been doing EA's *Music Construction Set*, a neat little program that competed successfully with ours.

"This is interesting," he said. "I have been thinking that we needed to do another music program. Maybe *Ed Bogas' Music Machine* is just what we need."

"I'd love to demo it for you. When can I come by?" I asked.

"I've got a producer in mind for the project. His name is Hal Jordy. I'll have him give you a call and make all the arrangements. This has turned out to be a very interesting lunch."

Hal gave me a call that same day. We did the demonstration for EA within a week. It was an interesting experience. EA hadn't done a music program for years, so most of the people we were demonstrating for had the same concerns that all the other publishers had. Only this time, I had Stuart Bond on my side. What a difference.

We did the contract with EA. It looked like *Ed Bogas' Music Machine* would be published by the biggest entertainment software company in the world, Electronic Arts.

I was wrong again. We were two-thirds of the way through development when EA decided to cancel all creativity product both present and future. And I mean *all*. Not only did they cancel our music creativity program; they also cancelled all of their art programs.

There is no doubt that creativity is a harder sell. Sports titles are much easier. If you tell someone you're doing a new baseball game, you're never asked, "What does it do?"

It was a sad day for me when EA cancelled it's creativity product line. How I miss *Deluxe Paint*!

Fujitsu loved both *Heaven & Earth* and *Ed Bogas' Music Machine* (Yes, it did ship with that name...Ed resigned himself to the inevitability.) Satoh San's faith in us had been justified. They ended up producing two versions of each product, the full version with all of the features, and a light version designed for their new game machine.

Disney's versions of *Heaven & Earth* (PC and Mac) were moderately successful. They were still struggling with how to market interactive software successfully. It was a frustrating thing for them. They were so used to being the best at anything that had to do with consumer entertainment products. They went through three different executives in charge of computer software just during the time that *Heaven & Earth* was under development.

Like almost all of our product, *Heaven & Earth* got fantastic reviews, with comments like, "a masterpiece," or "the finest puzzle game...ever!" But more important, the people who purchased it loved it. It was everything that they hoped for when they picked it up off the shelf and took it to the register...this was always our goal, and we always reached it.

The best compliment I received on *Heaven and Earth*, came just recently. I was working for a company called Eclipse Entertainment doing the *Jack Nicklaus 5* computer golf game. We had hired a new programmer, Ken Baird, to work on the World Editor for our new 3D Engine. I was walking by his office a couple of days after he came to work for us, and he hollered out, "Brad!"

I stopped, stuck my head in his door, and answered, "Yeees?"

"Did you do *Heaven & Earth?*" he asked.

"Yes, I did!" I said.

"A good friend of mine was just up on our Website and saw where you were our VP of Product Development. He wanted me to find out if you were the same Brad Fregger who did *Heaven & Earth.*"

"There's not too many Brad Fregger's around," I said. "So your friend is one of the few who discovered *Heaven & Earth?*"

"More than that, he told me it was his favorite game of all time...that he purchased a new computer just so he could play it the way it was meant to be played. He asked me to thank you for developing it."

I don't care how old you get, or how many products you've produced...it always feels good to know your work has been appreciated.

What to do now? That was the question. I didn't have to wait long for the answer...Michael had another idea. I wondered where this one would take me.

Seize the Day!   Chapter 23

When we had been working with Accolade on *Ishido*, the marketing director, Jeff
Hoff, had been closely involved, taking *Ishido* on as a personal project. As a result,
Michael Feinberg and Jeff became very good
friends; and they began to plan the design,
development, marketing and sales of their
own product—a company of their own.

These are two of the most creative
people I have ever known. There was never
any doubt in my mind that the product
they would design would be something
very special.

Throughout the entire time I was producing *Ed Bogas' Music Machine*, I would
hear from Michael about the terrific product
he and Jeff were designing. He'd ask me to
come by and see the latest incarnation...or
evaluate the latest proposal.

The program they were working on was
a very special calendar program, one that
would have the person's calendar, their To
Do List, phone numbers and addresses, a
daily quote, a list of things that had happened today in history, a personal journal,
and gorgeous pictures from all over the
world. You really need to see this product to
understand it. They called it *Seize the Day!*

One day we were meeting and Michael

said, "Brad, you believe in what we're doing, don't you?"

"Sure I do. I have complete confidence that you two guys can come up with something wonderful," I said.

"We want more than your confidence...we want your commitment. We want you to produce it for us. Come on board as our Vice President of Product Development. And we want Ian and Mike to program it, plus Mark to do the artwork. Scott's going to help design it."

"That sounds like a great plan," I said. "But where are you going to get the money? None of us are going to work on spec. We never have...we never will."

"Don't worry, we'll get the money. I've already got some leads. In the meantime, I'm moving up to Calistoga and I want to call a preliminary design meeting up there. Can you come?" he asked.

"Sure. Who else is invited?" I asked.

"There'll be Jeff and myself, Mike, Ian, Scott, Mark, and you."

"That's quite a group...sounds like you're getting serious about *Seize the Day!*" I said.

"You bet we are!"

The initial design meeting at Michael's new home in Calistoga, a small town in California at the top of the Napa Valley wine country, went well. The company would be called Seize the Day, and it would have one major product to begin with, the *Seize the Day!* calendar program. But that wasn't all. They would also market a number of calendar "plug-ins" that would greatly enhance the value of the product. These would include picture libraries including the works of such famous classical artists as Maxfield Parrish and Salvadore Dali, fantasy artists like Boris Vallejo and Robert Venosa, photos by Trevor Watson and Paul B. Goode.

In addition, there would be daily quotes and messages from *Growing a Business* by Paul Hawken and *The Dream Journal & Symbol Dictionary* from Betty Bethards...and more...so much more. I didn't see how we could possibly get this all done in the time Michael was allotting, nine months from start to finish.

Michael also laid out the responsibilities for everyone:

Michael and Jeff were sharing the management of the company. Michael was also in charge of all of the plug-in art, including any preparation needed for it to be included in the program. Jeff would have responsibility for all text material, i.e. the daily quotes, history notations, etc.

Scott Kim would have the major responsibility for designing the personal organizer and would do the initial design on the Macintosh in Hypercard.

Mark Ferrari would do the main art for the calendar program, beautiful pictures original to *Seize the Day!*.

Ian Gilman would do the "Gallery" programming, the part of the program that displayed the pictures.

Mike Sandige would do the programming for the "Personal Organizer" part of the program, the part that contained the calendar, lists, etc.

And I would produce the entire project, be responsible for making sure that we stayed on schedule and came out at the end with a product that worked together well.

When it was all done, Jeff and Mike would share in the responsibility of marketing and selling it. Jeff, most recently the Director of Marketing for Accolade, seemed more than qualified to take on this task.

When we left the meeting, we were all pumped about being involved in such a special project. I didn't think I could be surprised by anything else...I was wrong.

Back at the hotel, Ian, Mike and Mark began to talk about their plan for "Living Worlds." The idea was that Mark's artwork would be continually changing. He would have one basic scene for each month, but that scene would evolve as the day progressed. It would start out at dawn and go through the entire day, until it was night. Clouds would come and go, shadows would follow the sun, storms with lightning would move through the landscape. At night, the moon would rise, stars would fall...on and on.

"But how is this possible?" I asked. "It will take too much

memory to have all of those different images."

"We don't have different images," Mark answered. "We have only the basic image. All we do is change the color palette."

"I don't understand." I was feeling awfully dumb...not a good feeling when you're in charge of the project.

"Here, let me show you...come over to the window," Mark said. "Now see that view?" I nodded. "Imagine that that is one of my pictures...what's the color palette?"

It was night.

"Mostly different shades of gray and black," I said.

"Right! Now, when it's dawn the palette will change... right?" I nodded again. "But the scene itself won't change...right?"

It was finally beginning to make sense.

"So you mean...you will just change the color palette...we won't have to change the picture?"

"Yes."

"Is that possible?" I looked at Mike and Ian. They both nodded and Ian said, "It's really easy, at least theoretically...all we have to do is cycle the palette. We should be able to do it continuously. I doubt anyone will ever see it change; but when they come back an hour later, the picture will be completely different."

Then Mike added, "We may have to animate certain things, like the moon and the clouds, but that should be kept to a minimum. Nope, there's no reason why this shouldn't work."

"Do you have any idea how many effective images each scene will have?" I asked.

"If you mean how many different images, that's hard to calculate," Ian answered.

"Just give me a figure that would be fair...one that could be used in our PR campaign or in our advertising."

"It would be fair to say, 'over a million different images each month,'" Ian responded.

"This is fantastic. All this and animations too...Wow!

Dawn, dusk, nightfall, rain, waterfalls, ocean waves...all of this animating and changing continuously throughout the day. Tell me there has never been anything like this...tell me this is a first!"

"It's a first, Brad," Mike said laughingly. "But it's probably a last, too...we won't be able to do any of this if the computer's color palette is more than 256 colors. So as soon as it becomes common to use 16 to 32 bit color palettes, that's the end of the "Living Worlds.""

It's hard for me to believe that this conversation took place only six years ago, and already the 8 bit, 256 color palette is a thing of the past. Most computers today use a 32 bit color palette (effectively millions of colors). This sounds like an advance—in many ways it is— but it is also a loss, because now we can't cycle colors, now we can't see the "Living Worlds" of *Seize the Day!*

Michael was true to his word, and very quickly *Seize the Day!* had sufficient funding to take it well through its development stage. Paul Hawken, the founder of Smith & Hawken, as well as the author of *Growing a Business* (also a PBS special) joined the company and became the Chairman of its Board of Directors. In addition, a friend of his made a major investment in the company, as did Greg Walberg. Dick joined as Chief Financial Officer, which meant that Publishing International was put on hold for the foreseeable future.

Now, Seize the Day had a secure management team in place, money in the bank, and a product under development, with a promise to ship before the year was out. There was a lot of work yet to do.

All in all, the product development went according to schedule. At least the Personal Organizer did. Shortly into the project, Ian developed Carpal Tunnel Syndrome and couldn't use a keyboard anymore. He compensated by teaching his girlfriend, Sofie McKenzie, how to program, and she did a terrific job. But then they broke up, and things got a little dicey. But we still made it.

The other major problem was with the Macintosh. We had

already shipped to a major retail chain, when we discovered a fatal bug that trashed the user's data file. We had to recall everything, and I am sorry to say, we were never able to get it fixed. The only saving grace was that the bug only effected older Macs, which means the program works wonderfully well on my machine. I'm still using it...there is still not a calendar program on the market that comes anywhere near it as far as dependability, ease of use, efficiency, beauty, valuable features, etc.

And the "Living World's"...they worked out just as planned. They are a masterpiece of artistic skill. I don't think there is another artist in the world that could have accomplished what Mark did. He created twelve beautiful and original scenes; then he found out how to change the color palettes in the scenes to emulate the changing colors as the day moves from darkness to light and back to darkness. For October he added in the changing colors of the leaves. There was never anything like this before or since.

We were about two months from completion when it came to my attention that somebody needed to script the year. What I mean is, somebody had to tell the program when the sun would rise, when it would set, when a storm would develop, when lights in buildings would go on, when the moon would rise, when stars would fall, when it would snow, when the ghosts would come out (October had a haunted castle), when the leaves would turn, when the clouds would blow through, etc. In other words, somebody would have to play God.

That task fell to Danny Aldrich (Dick's son) and myself. It took the entire time we had available. I remember driving across the desert just after we had completed this massive task. The sun was rising, and there was a band of clouds on the horizon. I couldn't help but notice the similarity between what God had done, and what Danny and I had just finished doing. Our version didn't look nearly as good, but it was a passable replica.

Seize the Day! received hundreds of letters from satisfied customers, people who were blown away by the "the best personal organizer I have ever seen or used."

My favorite letter came from a lady who wrote,

> *"I spent the afternoon putting in all of my calendar information, phone numbers and addresses, and then playing around with the journal. During this whole time, I was captivated by the beautiful picture that included a mountain scene.*
>
> *"When I finished with my work, I decided to leave the computer on so I could enjoy the picture more. I did notice that as the day ended outside, the picture itself took on a different quality, almost like the day was ending in the computer world as well. But I figured that the effect was due to the changing light in my room, not to anything in the computer. How could the day end in the computer world? It didn't make any sense.*
>
> *"I sat down to read a magazine and glanced up every now and then to see the computer picture, as well as the beautiful view out my window, which coincidentally had a mountain in it too. Then I got the shock of my life...I noticed that outside my window the moon was just beginning to rise from behind the mountain...and in the computer scene, the moon was beginning to rise also. It was an eerie experience, both scary and wonderful at the same time. For just a moment I got confused as to which was the real, and which the computer, world.*
>
> *"Thank you, thank you, thank you for such a wonderful program. You have made my day...no more than that...I really don't have the words. Thanks again, Mary Smith."*

It was an exciting and affirming letter—a part of me believes that all our work was worth the joy, awe, and surprise we brought that one person.

Sales and marketing *is* the most difficult task of all. This is so hard to understand. Everyone thinks they are an expert when it comes to sales and marketing.

This is especially true if the person was involved in the sales and marketing effort for a major company. After all, they're responsible for the success they're experiencing. But the truth is, they're the lucky recipients of the marketing power the company has been able to garner over the years.

I only believe in an individual's capability when they have achieved marketing success for a brand new product, being offered by a brand new company. And then they are able to repeat their success with another new product, from another new company. This is the most difficult task of all.

I tried to warn Jeff and Michael that it was going to be different marketing *Seize the Day!*, that we wouldn't have the same advantages Jeff had when he had been with Accolade. I knew this from personal experience. I had been through the mill more than once. But this is a difficult concept for someone to handle. They *know* their previous success was due to *their* own skill. It should be easy to repeat that success with this new company, especially if the program was as wonderful as we planned it to be.

It's times like this that I hate to say, "I told you so." I would have much rather been wrong. I would have much rather that *Seize the Day!* had been a phenomenal success, with Mike and Jeff taking the credit for it. But it didn't work out that way; and even with a respectable "sell in," the "sell through" was slow and needed marketing help to get started.

The trouble was, by the time we discovered additional funds were needed, Seize the Day had gone through all of its initial investment capital; and Mike and Jeff, the major stockholders, weren't willing to bite the bullet and give up a major portion of the company to get more. They also passed up a couple of opportunities to license the product, because the price never seemed high enough.

There was no time to develop alternate plans; the money was gone and *Seize the Day!* died a quiet death.

Dr. Triguna, a well-known East Indian Ayur-Vedic physician, says and I paraphrase, "The god's are in charge of these six things: fame and infamy, wealth and poverty, and life and death."

We don't know why one movie becomes a fantastic hit, or why a piece of music, or a book, sells millions of copies. We don't know the formula for success...at least the formula that brings it when a major, multi-million dollar marketing effort isn't behind it. Somehow I think Dr. Triguna is right...the god's are in charge.

If this is so, what can you do? You can do what you must do—continue to create beautiful things. If the gods bless you, that's wonderful; you've won the lottery. If they don't, there's always the Mary Smiths. You know...that really *is* enough.

Beginning Again   Chapter 24

After the failure of *Seize the Day!* it became pretty obvious that Publishing International was not long for the world. It can take almost a year to complete contract negotiations on the development of an entertainment software product. During the year I spent with Seize the Day, I had not even looked for the next project. I suddenly realized that I was tired of all of that hassle.

Publishing International had a good run. We developed a lot of exceptional product, stayed healthy, and supported a number of people for almost ten years. But it was finally over.

What to do....

I wanted to do something different, maybe something easier than software development. One day in a bookstore I saw the audio book section. As I looked over the titles... maybe...why not! Time to *seize the moment*. I did some research, put together a business plan, and went to see Greg Walberg. As it turned out, he loved audio books and liked the idea of starting an audio book publishing company of his own. I would be the publisher as well as doing everything else needed to get the books ready for market.

That was how Parrot Audio Books was begun, how I began the adventure where

I met Burt Reynolds and John Denver and produced their autobiographies, how I worked with William Peter Blatty and produced the twenty-fifth anniversary editions of *The Exorcist*, as well as *Flowers for Algernon*...and how we found out that audio books might be easier to produce than computer software, but at least as hard to market. But that's another story, one that will have to wait for another book.

Late in 1995 we were ready to close down Publishing International for good, and we'd already quit producing new titles for Parrot Audio Books. All of a sudden, I found myself in the position of having to look for work. I needed to talk to someone so I could get my priorities straight. I called Ken Coleman, who by this time was one of the top executives at Silicon Graphics, a computer manufacturing company that had become a leader in the industry, especially in the area of producing leading-edge graphics workstations. Ken suggested we have breakfast together.

I went to see Ken because I needed someone I could trust to talk to. I wasn't sure whether I wanted to go back to software development, back to training and development, or on to something new. I felt that I had a lot to contribute to the right company. I was pretty sure there wasn't anyone better at getting things done and projects finished.

I thought the experience I had producing products and managing small teams, added to my previous experiences in training and development, would make me a very valuable resource to industry, especially the computer industry, hardware and software.

At breakfast Ken asked me what I'd been doing lately, and I told him about my past two years in the audio book business.

"You know as well as I do what two years means in the computer industry. It's the same as being ten years behind in any other field. As far as training goes, we're doing things here you never dreamed of. The World Wide Web has completely changed the face of training. It would be like you were starting over."

"You don't paint a very rosy picture," I said. "It's a little early for me to take out the golf clubs. In fact, I never plan on retiring. Do you think it's time for me to start a new career?"

"What do you know about the World Wide Web?" he asked.

"Only what I read in the newspapers."

"Well, it's going to be a major force in communication. Everyone will be involved someday. Since it's early yet, and there are a lot of small companies out there that will need help being brought up-to-date, you could start a Web services company. It might turn out to be pretty lucrative for you."

When I didn't respond, he continued, "I'll tell you what, you make an appointment with my VP of Personnel. He'll show you around, introduce you to my Director of Training and Development and maybe a couple of other people. You can see how we are using the World Wide Web here, see how you might be able to start up a small company to provide Web services to others or, maybe there's something here you can do that I'm not aware of."

This wasn't exactly what I had gone to Ken for, but the Web stuff sounded interesting, and just maybe there'd be something at Silicon Graphics for me. Although, I wasn't sure how happy I'd be working for a big company again. There's something about being in your own business that's extremely compelling.

Prior to the meetings, I called another good friend from the Activision days, Sherry Whiteley-Roach. She was Silicon Graphics' head of world-wide recruiting. But more important, Sherry had always liked me.

"You're going to interview here?" she asked.

"Well, he did say that there might be something at Silicon Graphics for me...but he also suggested I start a Web services company to service small business needs," I told her.

"You know Ken, he likes to cover the bases, doesn't like

to make any promises. I think it's great you're interviewing here. There are plenty of places that your knowledge can be used to our advantage. You'll like Silicon Graphics. It's your kind of company."

This was beginning to sound more promising.

She continued, "We have a division, Silicon Studios, whose responsibility it is to interface with the computer entertainment industry. They also have the responsibility of working with Hollywood, the motion picture industry; and that's where their major focus is. You could help out on the computer entertainment side. I'll make sure you get to talk to our person over there too."

"Sounds great. I'm sure glad I called you, Sherry. It's always wonderful talking to you."

The next day I met with the VP of Personnel. He was an intelligent guy, who seemed honestly interested in discussing possibilities. He also showed me their Web site and the way they were using it. There is no doubt that Silicon Graphics knew how to take advantage of the World Wide Web. This was over three years ago, and I still haven't seen a company doing it as well. What training I saw looked interesting, very much like the stuff I had experimented with when I was at Mervyn's fifteen years before. The only difference was I had been using a system called Plato, and they were using the World Wide Web, which hadn't existed at that time.

I began to focus on the computer entertainment division; if I had any chance to join Silicon Graphics, it was there. Ken had mentioned in our conversation that he thought before long all entertainment software development would be done on Silicon Graphics machines. At the time he said this, I wondered how much I *had* missed in two years.

Publishing International had considered using Silicon Graphics machines in the past, had even come close to doing some demos for them to show off their machines. None of these deals ever made it to the development stage; but some had gotten pretty close, one close enough that they had loaned us a machine to begin work on, to evaluate its capability of doing the kinds of demos that we were good at. While we agreed they were fast and much more powerful than the PC's were at that time, we were always disappointed in the tools available. My top programmers made it clear they believed, that overall, the PC was a better platform for games development.

I decided I needed to do some research. I called the top product development people in the industry and asked them what was happening in product development, especially in regard to preferred platforms for software development and the state of the Silicon Graphics machines in this regard. Everyone told me the same thing. They had always preferred the tools on the PC, while envying the power of the Silicon Graphics machines. What had changed was that the Silicon Graphics tools were not any better, while the power of the PC was increasing dramatically. It was no longer a race...the PC had won.

"What about Nintendo? Don't they have some sort of a deal with them?" I'd ask.

"There's a problem there. The development systems are very expensive; and more and more developers are finding it easier and faster to work on PC's. They're beginning to wonder why they're spending all that money for a system that doesn't give them everything they need to do the job."

Then I had the chance to interview for the VP of Product Development of one of the top video/computer game companies in the Silicon Valley. When I went for the interview, the current VP bragged about their use of Silicon Graphics machines.

"Everyone of our artists has one," he said. "This is how we do our state-of-the-art work."

"Could I talk with them?" I asked.

"Sure, come on, let's go back to the lab so you can talk with the artists."

After introducing me around, he left me alone so I walked into the first artist's cubical and asked, "I see you have two machines here, a PC and a Silicon Graphics. How do you like the Silicon Graphics machine?"

"I love it, it's the main reason I came here, so I could figure out how it worked, and make some real cool stuff."

"It is a terrific machine, isn't it? Which one do you do most of the real work on?"

"Oh, the PC. There's not much I can do on the Silicon Graphics machine. The tools make it difficult to work fast enough. We have to really put out the work here."

I went from cubical to cubical asking the same questions and getting the same answers. I don't think the VP of Product Development even knew those machines weren't being used, or cared for that matter. As a perk, they had gotten him a fine team of artists; they probably paid for themselves on that alone.

The exciting thing was, I had figured out how I could honestly help Silicon Graphics. Their machines were obviously loved for their power. The problem was the tools weren't good enough to compete with the PC; and people really weren't sure how they could use them to their advantage, or if they were worth the extra money. What Silicon Graphics needed was an computer games evangelist. Now, this I could do. I was probably one of the of best people in the world for this job. I went to my interview confident that I had done my research, that I was ready.

⁂

The interview was a disaster from the beginning.

"Who are you and why am I talking to you?" were the first words out of the young Personnel Director's mouth.

I was caught by surprise; I had thought that she would have at least read my resumé. "I'm Brad Fregger, a friend of Ken's. I'm here to interview for a position with Silicon Studios," I said.

"I scanned your resumé. What on earth do you think you could do for us?" she said.

"I have spent quite a few years in the computer entertainment industry. I know that you are focused on the movie business, but your charter includes the computer entertainment business. And I think you might need some help there," I said as carefully as possible.

"What do you mean, we "need some help there"? We own the most significant part of that business; aren't you aware of our relationship with Nintendo? What we don't own now, we will in a couple of years. Didn't you do some research before coming to see me?" The last comment was not a question. This was not going well.

"The research that I did do suggested that your tools might not be up to par...that an evangelist into the software development community might be a very good idea." I said, still trying to get the conversation on track.

"I don't have time to talk with you, even if you are a friend of Ken Coleman's. This interview is over." And she got up and left the small conference room we were in.

I had told her the truth, but I guess she wasn't ready to hear it. Within a short couple of years, they were in trouble, struggling for survival. They ended up losing market share very quickly to the PC, especially as the PC's power increased even faster than anyone dreamed possible. Without the tools, they didn't have a chance to compete in the computer entertainment arena.

Even if they had hired me, I don't believe I could have gotten the tools developed in time...it was already too late. I'm really sorry this happened. Silicon Graphics is a great company; they just couldn't see the dangers that lay ahead of them. But then, I have already said that the ability to see that the world is passing you by is one of the most difficult things for a senior executive to do. Facing potential dangers, facing our fears, is always hard but critical for long-term success.

Final Thoughts

Chapter 25

Even though my meetings at Silicon Graphics had turned out to be disastrous, they had resulted in my becoming very interested in the Internet and the World Wide Web. I saw another opportunity to *seize the moment* and by early 1996, I had formed a new company, Groundbreaking Productions. Soon I had four registered domains and was providing Web and Internet Services to other small businesses.

The Internet and the World Wide Web fascinated me. As a futurist I knew that I was involved in one of those special moments when the world and the way it works changes. There was no doubt that this was a new communications paradigm, one at least as significant as the printing press.

Before the printing press, communications were fairly limited, individuals talked one-on-one, and very few people communicated beyond a relatively small circle. With the development of the printing press, it became possible for one person to have much greater influence, and we entered the age of one communicating with the many. Radio, movies, and television didn't change that...it was still one communicating with the many.

Now we have the World Wide Web. No

longer do we have the one communicating with the many; now we have the many communicating with the many, and this will change the world! How it will change it, whether it will be changed for better or for worse, will have to be judged by future generations...but it will be changed.

There's an old Chinese curse, "May you be born in interesting times." We have all been *cursed*, as there have never been more interesting times; and we have all been *blessed* to be a part of it.

I love the Web! I love how I can share myself and my interests with others, and they can share themselves and their interests with me. On my personal Website I have a photo gallery of outstanding pictures from outer space (taken by the different NASA voyages). Anyone can come visit my photo gallery and look at my pictures—*anyone in the world*. But it's better than that. If someone sees a picture they like, they can take it with them. And, just like a smile, I can give it away and still have it. I can give it away a million times, and I will still have it. I love that!

⟨ ⟩

I have been able to spend most of my life working with motivated, committed people who are dedicated to getting the job done and getting it done well. As I was writing this book and thinking back over the years, remembering the people I worked with, the lessons I learned, and the things we accomplished, I have been reminded once more just how lucky I have been.

Ron Berlin at Atari gave me responsibility and opportunity to develop the confidence I needed to accomplish the seemingly impossible.

Ken Coleman challenged me in more ways than I care to remember. He made me become all that I could become— he demanded it of me. But he was always there when I faltered, always there when I exposed my weak underbelly.

There were others during those Activision days: Tom Lopez's wisdom, Dick Lehrberg's patience, Brodie Lockard's inspiration, David Crane's graciousness, the commitment of the entire internal development group.

When we started Publishing International, there was the wonderful support of my wife, Kathie, my friends, Dick and Diana Aldrich, Tom and Dorothy Sunday, the friendship and creative genius of Michael Feinberg, and our Japanese agent, Jan Putman. There were also the highly skilled and committed development teams who were motivated to make the finest products in the world: Brodie Lockard, Mike Sandige, Ian Gilman, Ed Bogas, Greg Hospelhorn, Mark Ferrari, Scott Kim, John Blu, John Keene, and Ivan and Carol Manley. And, of course, there were my friends and associates, Gilman Louie and Phil Adam.

In Japan, there was Yoshihiro Satoh and Takashi Ochiai of Fujitsu Limited and Hiro of Acclaim, who showed me business can be honorable, promises and commitment can be depended upon.

Then there were the two whose financial support and belief in me made it all possible, Tom Randolph and Greg Walberg. How wonderful they were, never faltering in their continued long-term support.

These were the people. Our accomplishments included some of the best video games of all time: *Pitfall II*, *Ghostbusters*, *Shanghai* and *Solitaire Royale*; *Hometown, U.S.A.*; *Ishido*; *Heaven & Earth*; *Ed Bogas' Music Machine*; and *Jack Nicklaus 5 Computer Golf*...over one hundred products in all.

What a blessing to have been a significant part of this, to have been able to work with these wonderful people, to have accomplished all of this since my fortieth birthday. What a blessing indeed!

Afterword

Up in Seattle, Washington, lives an inspiring individual who isn't particularly well known to the general population. His name is Dale Chihuly, and he's perhaps the greatest glass artist of the twentieth century.

Individual Chihuly pieces command as much as $60,000, with multiple piece works selling for six-figure sums. His creations can be found in New York's Metropolitan Museum of Art, the Smithsonian's Renwick Gallery, and over eighty other museums here and abroad. He is also one of the rare American artists to have had a solo show at the Louvre.

At the height of his career, in 1976, Chihuly was involved in an automobile accident that caused total blindness in his left eye. The resulting loss of depth perception made it all but impossible for him to blow glass. This should have meant the end of his career, could have meant a life spent living with regret and "the unfairness of it all."

It didn't. Since he couldn't blow, he taught others to, and then to create glass art to his specifications. Dale Chihuly's work continues; his studio in Seattle is still producing the finest glass art in the world.

Chihuly not only *seized the moment* after

his accident, he seizes it every day in the way that he works with the men and women who make up his team.

"I rely heavily on the intuition of my craftsmen," he says. "It would be a mistake to try to exert too much control, I think it would kill a vital spark. Chance is a crucial ingredient—the unpredictability of the glass, of the colorist, of the gaffers. My job is to be a catalyst—to set the wheels in motion, keep the energy level high, and let things happen. I love how every time these oven doors open you're presented with another surprise."

⬤⬤⬤

This is often the experience when we are able to let things happen, get out of the way, *seize the moment*. The end is always a surprise, always something different, often something better than we originally planned.

But *seizing the moment* takes practice, it takes commitment, decision, courage to face the unfaceable, faith that you can deal with it, whatever it is, one day, one hour, one moment at a time! Sometimes it takes knowing you are not alone, that there are others that care, whether you are aware of them or not. Christians believe that Jesus is with them all of the time. Hindus believe in a supreme consciousness, manifested in many different gods. All of the great religions know there is something beyond this life, this world. How else do you explain synchronicity? How else do you explain serendipity? How else do you explain the unexplainable?

There are things you can do to make yourself more sensitive, more aware, more capable of accepting the inexplicable into your life.

You begin by *becoming sensitive to your own intuition*, to the cues in your life that you need to do something, do something different, do something unexpected. These cues come at different times for different reasons. They come at different times for different people.

You might be walking down the street, or having a cup of coffee with a business associate, and a thought comes to mind. For just a moment you feel you need to respond in some way. And then just as quickly, it's *out* of your mind, and you forget it until something happens and you remember. And then it's too late! You need to train yourself to become sensitive to these cues, in both your business and your personal life.

I call this becoming "cue sensitive" and it's a skill I teach to managers in my leadership classes. It is an essential skill for any manager, especially if they are expected to accomplish difficult things. Anyone can learn to be "cue sensitive" and find it highly valuable as they learn to live successfully in this world.

You might have an intuitive flash in the middle of the night, or just upon waking, or while taking your shower. The trick is to take these flashes *seriously*. Write them down. Act on them immediately, treat them with respect. This is the beginning of learning the skill of *seizing the moment*.

<hr/>

I started writing this book in the middle of June, 1998. I had thought about it for years, even written some preliminary chapters. I wanted it to be a selection of stories from my life. I had discovered that personal stories can be very impactual and I had a lot of them. Prior to this writing stint, I would have judged myself to be a fairly average writer. I've always been a good storyteller, but I knew I was better orally than in writing.

Something happened this time. The writing came easy, seemed almost inspired. I was working full time. Yet I would wake up at four in the morning with a whole chapter in my head, come to my computer, and have it written before seven. The first draft of *Lucky That Way* was completed by the middle of August.

After finishing, I passed it around to a number of different people; this was my "beta test." I discovered just telling stories left some people confused. They needed something to hold it all together. Then it dawned on me that I could add to the book my philosophy of "*seizing the moment.*" This would let me share just how *seizing the moment* has worked in my life and my work, and it would be the golden thread that held it all together.

It's very interesting how consciously involving yourself in this type of thinking causes things to happen. Since this was my first book, I was concerned about finding a publisher. I know of many people who have finished books and never found a publisher.

I was preparing a media blitz designed to find the right publisher (one who liked my style of writing, was big enough to have books in all of the major retailers, yet small enough so my book would be important), when my fiancée, Barbara Foley, told me that she wanted me to go to Iowa with her to visit family and friends.

I was too busy; I had a book to get published! I told her I would go, but I had to work while we traveled. She mentioned that she knew a publisher in Iowa who might be interested in my book.

This publisher was in a small town we were going to be visiting, so Barbara called and made an appointment for me to meet with the managing editor, Rodney Charles. I sent him my book and checked him out on the Web. It looked like a waste of time; the Website's url was newagepage.com. This didn't feel right for a book on the computer games industry. I was in for a surprise!

Rodney and I met a few days after we arrived in town. The first thing he did was show me one of his current books, *The Official Video Game & Pinball Book of World Records.* He said the book was getting lots of press and that most of it was around a small section in the book that talked about the history of video games.

He was excited about the possibility of publishing my book. We talked further and I discovered that he liked my style of writing, had published about fifty books, and had distribution in all of the major retailers. This was truly *serendipity!* I set off for one destination and arrived someplace totally unexpected, someplace more wonderful than I could have dreamed of. Within a half hour, we had made a deal and I had my publisher.

Now I had to find someone to write the foreword. I put together a list of possibilities with my dream candidate at the top. This was *Orson Scott Card*, my favorite science fiction/fantasy writer. I knew he was interested in computer games, wrote the Gameplay Column in *Compute!* magazine, but I hesitated to ask him. I figured he must be terribly busy. It would take four to five weeks for him to answer, and then he'd probably say no. And I'd be right back where I started.

Barbara entered the picture again, "I thought you were writing a book about *seizing the moment?*"

I went right to my computer and sent a message to his Website. Then I prepared myself to wait patiently.

The next morning I got the answer, "OSC will definitely write the foreword...please send your book."

So the miracles keep coming, and *coincidence, synchronicity*, and *serendipity* keep playing a big role in my life. Believe me when I tell you, they can play a role in your's too. All you have to do is learn to *seize the moment!*

I love haiku poetry...probably because it reflects so well the concept of *seizing the moment*. One of my favorites was written by the haiku poet, Ryusui; it speaks to life as I have often experienced it...it speaks of *seizing the moment*.

> A lost child crying
> stumbling over
> the dark fields
> catching fireflies

Remember to *seize the moment* every chance you have!

THE END

Brad Fregger has 45 years experience in teaching (university level), retailing, corporate training, software development, and publishing. He has worked in large and small companies, started three of his own businesses, and worked as a senior executive in two other startups. He is currently president/CEO of Groundbreaking Press, a boutique book publishing company. Additionally, Brad is a lecturer (professor) at Texas State University-San Marcos (business communications and management).

Brad taught graduate-level courses at Saint Edward's University in Austin, Texas for over five years, including one year (2002) as the Executive in Residence for the Graduate School of Management. He founded the Corporate Training Departments of three major corporations (Mervyn's Department Stores, Atari Corporation, and Activision Corporation).

Brad has amassed a remarkable record of accomplishment over the past 45 years. He has produced more than 50 videos, 12 audio books, over 100 consumer and business enterprise software products, including the most successful computer game in the world (*Shanghai*) and the most played computer game in the world (computer card solitaire), and edited and published over 60 books on a wide variety of subjects.

Brad is an expert in many critical areas of business from customer service to the management of technology. He's an international speaker providing programs to major companies throughout the Middle East (Tunisia, Dubai, Beirut, Bahrain, Kuwait, and Qatar), Europe, and Canada in a broad spectrum of subjects. As an author he's written seven books, *GET THINGS DONE - Ten Secrets of Creating and Leading Exceptional Teams; ONE SHOVEL FULL - Telling Stories to Change Beliefs, Attitudes, and Perceptions; LUCKY THAT WAY - Stories of Seizing the Moment While Creating the Games Millions Play; WHY PUBLISH - Making the Right Choices for Your Book; MY THINKING CAP - Solutions for Global Crisis; GET OUT OF THE WAY – You'll Never Manage Your Way to Great Leadership;* and *WHY DOES ANYBODY BELIEVE IN GOD? – An Essay on Creation.*

In addition, Brad has published articles in professional journals, including articles for three highly respected online blogs: *American Thinker, America's Right,* and the *Moral Liberal.*

Brad's amazing ability to complete projects on time and on budget, plus his creative management style, caught the attention of Tom Peters (*In Search of Excellence*), who then featured Brad in his book, *Liberation Management.*

Brad holds a Master's Degree in Futuristics (San Jose State University). His speech, "Earthward Implications of Cosmic Migration," was given at the American Astronautical Society's proceedings in honor of the tenth anniversary of Apollo 11's landing on the moon.

Brad and his wife and business partner, Barbara Foley, live in the Texas hill country South of Austin.

www.ingramcontent.com/pod-product-compliance
Lightning Source LLC
Chambersburg PA
CBHW051231050326
40689CB00007B/882